1/04

Invest in your future with City and Guilds

City and Guilds, the UK's best known provider of vocational qualifications, has a long history of providing qualifications for Her Majesty's Armed Forces and can help you make the successful transfer from military to civilian life.

City and Guilds

■ **offers internationally recognised qualifications in over 400 subjects** – there are schemes suitable for recruits, trainees and other serving personnel, equipping them with the skills and qualifications they need

■ **issues the greatest number of National Vocational Qualifications (NVQs)** – NVQs define the skills or competences required in employment and prove to a civilian employer that your skills are transferable to the workplace

■ **promotes the use of Accreditation of Prior Learning (APL)** – APL enables you to be given credit for the skills you already have and can be used to claim exemption from parts of other qualifications

■ **has a progressive structure of awards** – if you already hold a Level 3 City and Guilds certificate you may be eligible for the award of Licentiateship (LCGI), the first in a scale of senior awards comprising Graduateship, Membership and Fellowship.

For more information about how City and Guilds can help you, please contact your Unit Resettlement Officer or

Services Liaison Officer
City and Guilds of London Institute
46 Britannia Street, London WC1X 9RG.

Tel: 071-278 2468   Fax: 071-278 9460

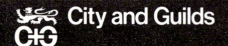

THE JOB ASSAULT COURSE

Get out and achieve your own goals

Opportunities Nationwide

The world of financial direct sales is a hard, competitive marketplace. For people with the will to succeed, it's an opportunity to carve your own career.

Norwich Union Private Clients is a brand new venture with a self-employed sales force that is growing daily. To join it you don't need to be a salesman. We're looking for people who can show success in a previous career, people with self-motivation and determination, people ready to change direction and capitalise on their experience.

We won't expect you to make the change all on your own — no team can function effectively without solid initial and ongoing training; Norwich Union will provide it.

We'll also give you a superb range of products — life plans, pensions, mortgages — all highly competitive and highly attractive.

We'll back you up with a dedicated Administration Unit, so that every move you make is fully supported and quickly serviced.

The rewards? That's up to you, but we know you can achieve all of your goals with the right attitude and the right handling.

For an evaluation of your potential with Norwich Union Private Clients phone Wendy Brownlie on 0603 687679

Norwich Union is an equal opportunities employer and welcomes applications from registered disabled persons

THE JOB ASSAULT COURSE

A Guide to Civilian Employment for Service Personnel

M C Lindsay Stewart

This book is dedicated to those who serve and to Connie without whose encouragement this book would never have been finished.

First published in 1992

Apart from any fair dealing for the purposes of research or private study, or criticism or review, as permitted under the Copyright, Designs and Patents Act, 1988, this publication may only be reproduced, stored or transmitted, in any form or by any means, with the prior permission in writing of the publishers, or in the case of reprographic reproduction in accordance with the terms of licences issued by the Copyright Licensing Agency. Enquiries concerning reproduction outside those terms should be sent to the publishers at the undermentioned address:

Kogan Page Limited
120 Pentonville Road
London N1 9JN

© M C Lindsay Stewart 1992

British Library Cataloguing in Publication Data

A CIP record for this book is available from the British Library.

ISBN 0-7494-0859-6

Typeset by DP Photosetting, Aylesbury, Bucks
Printed and bound in Great Britain by
Clays Ltd, St Ives plc.

Contents

Foreword   7
by General Sir Peter Inge, Chief of the General Staff

1. **Introduction**   9

2. **Before the Search Begins**   12
   The Fears *13*
   The Military Approach – The Appreciation *13*
   Self-analysis – Transferable Skills *19*
   Threat Analysis – Summing Up the Opposition *25*
   Preparation for Planning *26*

3. **Creating the Framework**   31
   The Network *31*
   The Rings of Confidence *31*

4. **Baiting the Hook: The Curriculum Vitae and Marketing Letter**   34
   Reason and Purpose of a CV *34*
   The Marketing Letter *41*

5. **Putting the Plan into Operation**   47
   The Execution of the Plan *47*
   Where the Jobs Are *48*
   The Human Resource Trap *61*
   Summary *67*

6. **Keeping Track of Your Job Search Campaign** 68
   Files 68
   Network Cards 69
   Thank You Letters 70

7. **Preparing for and Conducting the Interview** 73
   Following Up Your Letters by Telephone 73
   Getting Past the Secretary 74
   Preparing for the Interview 75

8. **The Interview** 84
   Pre-interview Action 85
   Introductions and Preliminaries 86
   The Interview 87
   Closing the Interview 89
   Post-interview Action 90
   Interview Techniques 92

9. **Dealing with Depression and Kick Starting a Stalled Search** 96
   Dealing with Depression 96
   Kick Starting a Stalled Search 99

10. **The Negotiations, the Offer and the Signing** 102
    Negotiations 102
    The Offer 106
    The Signing 108

11. **The First Few Months in the Job** 113

Bibliography 117

Foreword

by General Sir Peter Inge, Chief of the General Staff, GCB

The assault course is one of the earlier physical challenges in a Service career; the soldier, sailor or airman is trained to take it in his stride. It is an early and deliberate taste of the many challenges to surmount in a military career usually unpredictable in their nature but met face to face at sea, on land and in the air by those who have justifiably been called 'the best trained workforce in Britain'.

Those leaving the Services face a new and rather different assault course when they move to a second career in civilian life. But they take with them highly valuable skills, moulded by a programme of training, experience and assessment, into this new and, for most, unfamiliar environment. However, I am confident that the personal qualities and skills of Servicemen and women have much to offer a very wide range of civilian employers.

Michael Lindsay Stewart is one who has successfully tackled this challenge. In this book he analyses the process and offers some straightforward and simple advice in how personal energy and determination can be harnessed in the job hunt. In the Armed Forces we constantly contribute to corporate tasks; loyalty and teamwork lie at the heart of our ethos. At the end of a military career a great deal of help and advice for the transition to a second career is offered but ultimately taking one's skills into the market place is a private undertaking, in which success is mutually beneficial for those leaving the Service and potential employers.

I am delighted to introduce Michael's book, targeted to help those tackling the Job Assault Course.

CHAPTER 1
Introduction

To many civilians the world inhabited by those in uniform is both strange and divorced from their own. Of course, there are some aspects of the military whose direct application to the corporate world is obvious; the Gulf Conflict of 1990/91 is such a case in point. The bringing together of such a vast supply of men, women and materiel is an obvious distribution miracle, employing the highest standards of Just-in-Time (JIT) planning and coordination. Similarly, the daily briefings that we all watched were superb examples of marketing and sales presentation. However, for most in the corporate world, the mind image of those in uniform is formed from old-fashioned notions and a plethora of bad films. In essence:

> 'Military man – umm – well, there is leadership of course and he can organize tanks, but what can he do for me?'

The man in uniform is, of course, just as biased, blinkered and ignorant of his opposite number in the business world. Have you ever heard these words?

> 'He's something in the City.'
> 'Of course he's in trade.'
> 'All that company needs is some proper organization.'
> 'How in heaven's name did he get to be where he is?'

Yet in very many ways managers, both in and out of uniform, face the same problems:

- Recruiting, training and retaining skilled workers.
- Improving efficiency.
- Improving effectiveness.
- Re-equipping and updating.
- Presenting, to the public, a face of efficiency, effectiveness and competition.
- Satisfying their boss, his boss and ultimately the shareholders (the public).
- Finding solutions to problems.
- Strategic planning.
- Adapting to the changing marketplace (changing circumstances).

If this book promotes a better understanding of each other between managers in and out of uniform it will have been, in part, successful.

The Aim

The purpose of this guide is to make the transition to the world outside the service easier, by preparing for the obstacles in the Job Assault Course.

CHAPTER 2
Before the Search Begins

Your previous career will not have prepared you to job hunt. You will, probably, not have built up the contacts and connections which sustain those who are merely seeking a new position.

While the Services have not prepared the individual for changing careers, what it has given you is the authority, confidence, personality and practical approach to problem solving which will enable you to tackle that challenge.

You have a brain which has been trained to solve problems through analysis and logic. Gut instinct has been tempered with the ability to judge the other options and success has been brought about through careful planning, motivation and leadership.

These are equally highly prized skills in the civilian world. Do not sell yourself short; instead, apply these skills, as outlined in this book, and you will make the transition successfully out of the uniform into the suit.

Well, the decision has been made. It may have been by choice or because of the changing political shape of the world. Whatever, you are not committed to change. If you have been in the Services this is really nothing new; you have probably changed jobs every two to three years anyway. 'Ah, but it has always been with the same firm', I can visualize you saying. True, but the whole world has changed in the last decade. Lawyers and bankers, brokers and the executives of large conglomerates have all had to adjust to the new world order and recession. This is the chance to do something new, to grasp your life and direct its course. The first act is to deal with the fear of the unknown.

The Fears

The fears listed below beset all who face this task:

- What can I do?
- What do I do?
- Who wants me?
- How and where do I live?
- What will my friends say?

These are real fears, but many are unfounded. You can do whatever you want to, even become a brain surgeon if time, money, determination and commitments allow. But for most, these fears are dispelled when you employ the skills that you have been taught, when you analyse your *Transferable Skills* and prepare your *Campaign Plan*.

The Military Approach – The Appreciation

Situation analysis
This, the first analysis, is critical to your future planning. Remember, always account for the worst situation. Times at present are tough for all and while the future looks brighter than the recent past, you are preparing for a campaign within which there will be a number of skirmishes and battles. Prepare for a campaign which may last over a year. Take a large piece of paper and realistically write down your present situation, analysed under the following headings.

Financial analysis
List on one side all your income – private, family, Government, allowances and benefits. (Seek advice on all the allowances that you might claim – there are usually more

than you think. Do not be too proud to claim; you have paid for them and you are entitled to them.) Next, note when each item will alter or cease during the year. Some benefits will cease but your tax situation will also change.

On the other side of the paper list all your outgoings. *Do not cheat.* If you do a lot of entertaining, eating out or hobbies list their cost; don't dismiss them at this stage for it will only cause confusion within the family and to yourself. Now, total the outgoings and separate them into categories that you and your spouse deem Vital, Important, Desirable and Luxury.

Investigate the imponderable. Are you getting relocation assistance? If not, you will have to pay to get home. Do you have possessions in storage? You will have to pay to keep them in, or pay to get them out. Do you have somewhere to live? If so, remember to subtract the rent you were getting and to include the mortgage and associated costs. If not, research the area where you plan to live and include those costs. But remember, your place of residence will be influenced by the domestic analysis outlined below. Does your resettlement training have hidden costs? Do you have to pay for part of the resettlement course offered?

The analysis in Figure 1 will give some guidance. It is not definitive, as everyone has different financial situations, circumstances and priorities. It should, however, serve as a template.

Investigate the restructure of your assets and debts and restructure your insurance. Your bank manager and the other professionals are used to this; they will respect your professionalism and, almost without exception, will offer good advice.

Finally, balance your account and prepare your budget for a year. If you are in the black, great. If it's touch and go or in the red do your cost-cutting now.

FINANCIAL ANALYSIS
Income

Item	Value	Month	Year	Starts	Ends
BANK ACCOUNTS					
Current Account	xxx				
Savings Account	xxx				
Interest		xxx	xxx		
SHARES PORTFOLIO (last year average)					
Name	xxx		xxx		
Name	xxx		xxx		
Name	xxx		xxx		
TRUST FUNDS					
Name			xxx		
Name			xxx		
HOUSE RENTAL		xxx	xxx		
PAY					
Monthly		xxx	xxx	xxx	xxx
Terminal Grant	xxx				
Commutation	xxx				
Pension		xxx	xxx	xxx	
Redundancy Payment	xxx				
FAMILY					
Allowances		xxx	xxx	xxx	xxx
Unemployment Benefit		xxx		xxx	xxx
OTHER ALLOWANCES					
TOTAL	xxx	xxx	xxx		

Figure 1 *Financial Analysis*

EXPENDITURE

Item	Value	Month	Year	Starts	Ends
STAPLES					
Food (average)		xxx	xxx		
Clothing					
You		xxx	xxx		
Spouse		xxx	xxx		
Children		xxx	xxx		
School		xxx	xxx		
Heating (average)		xxx	xxx		
Electricity (average)		xxx	xxx		
Telephone		xxx	xxx		
HOUSING					
Rent		xxx	xxx		
Rates/Charges		xxx	xxx		
Maintenance		xxx	xxx		
Other Utilities		xxx	xxx		
SCHOOLING					
Fees			xxx		
Extras			xxx		
PETS					
Feed		xxx	xxx		
Vet (average)			xxx		
Quarantine		xxx		xxx	xxx
ENTERTAINMENT					
TV		xxx	xxx		
Cinema/Live		xxx	xxx		
Books/Magazines		xxx	xxx		
Dining Out (present average)		xxx	xxx		
Entertaining		xxx	xxx		
Drink		xxx	xxx		
Smoking		xxx	xxx		
Hobbies		xxx	xxx		
Club Membership			xxx		
Holidays			xxx		

Figure 1 *(Continued)*

ANNUAL EXPENSES					
Birthday Presents			xxx		
Christmas			xxx		
TRANSPORT					
Car Tax			xxx		
Car Maintenance			xxx		
Petrol		xxx	xxx		
Public Transport		xxx	xxx		
Air		xxx	xxx		
Rail		xxx	xxx		
BUSINESS EXPENSES					
Membership Fees			xxx		
Office Equipment	xxx				
Stationery		xxx	xxx		
Stamps		xxx	xxx		
Newspapers		xxx	xxx		
Dry-Cleaning		xxx	xxx		
INSURANCE					
Household (Building)		xxx	xxx		
Household (Contents)		xxx	xxx		
Life		xxx	xxx		
Private Medical		xxx	xxx		
Car		xxx	xxx		
DEBTS					
Overdraft	xxx	xxx	xxx	xxx	xxx
Mortgage	xxx	xxx	xxx	xxx	xxx
Finance Company	xxx	xxx	xxx	xxx	xxx
Credit Card	xxx	xxx	xxx		

SUB TOTAL   xxx

ANNUAL INCOME   xxx

ANNUAL EXPENDITURE   xxx

BALANCE =   xxx

divide by 12 = £   = Net Montly Income/(Excess Expenditure)

Figure 1 *(Continued)*

Domestic analysis
Everyone's domestic circumstances are different but remember that what you do will affect others and you will need the planning team of your family. So analyse your domestic situation.

- Where are the children at school?
- Is their stability at present critical?
- Does your spouse work?
- Is that career stability critical?
- Do you have dependants who need your close presence?
- Does the location of your residence limit your mobility?
- Is there anywhere you would not move to?
- Why?

The result of this analysis will provide a template which will show you just how widespread a campaign you can conduct. In military parlance, it is the consideration of the ground. The greater the limitations on mobility, the greater the limitations on the plan.

Mission analysis
The reason for this analysis is to determine exactly what your mission is. At first this may seem simple. 'My mission is to secure a job.' Even for the most desperate of job seekers such a statement cannot be true. What about some limitations to that mission, ie:

My mission is to secure a(n)   self-satisfying / honest / enjoyable / worthwhile / well-paid / pleasurable / respectable / suitable / promotable / hardworking / less stressful   job.

Again, get out the pad and list all those things that you have ever done and really enjoyed, and keep on asking yourself, why? Then list all those things that you have not enjoyed. Again keep asking yourself, why? Now get your spouse to do the same exercise. (Remember that this is a planning team; no great leader has planned a campaign by himself.)

The next step is for you both, separately, to list all those things that you could not countenance for social, moral, ethical or religious reasons.

'Think these exercises sound like time wasting? Well, consider your attitude to these scenarios:'

1. Working for a property development firm which makes its money from buying up defaulted mortgages, repossessing the property and then letting to tenants.
2. Administering a chain of private abortion clinics.
3. Working in a closed, strict Muslim country.
4. Managing the estate, in a remote part of Scotland, for an absentee landlord.
5. Commuting overseas for five days each week.
6. Working in an office with a strict hierarchy and autocratic management, or its converse.

The answers that each one of you gives will differ, but they do provide a clue to what type of job would satisfy you. A highly successful book which gives guidance on in-depth self-analysis is *What Color is your Parachute?* by Richard Nelson Bolles.

With these exercises completed you should now be able to define your *mission*.

Self-analysis - Transferable Skills

This analysis will determine the type of job that you can apply for with a chance of being considered. If your previous analytical exercises have shown that something new and completely different is what will satisfy your family, the course to follow must be to go back to school and retrain. If, like the majority, you enjoyed much of what you did before, here is where you define your well-earned experience and skills and translate them into those skills that an employer can relate to and use. *Remember the words – relate to and use.*

If at the end of this six-stage analysis you have not covered the best part of ten pages of foolscap paper, you have cheated yourself.

Stage 1

Take your page and divide it in three vertically. Starting when you were at school, or if over 30, at university or on enlistment or commissioning, write a heading to cover the first two-year period (see Figure 2). Write down everything that you were responsible for or achieved including:

People	Hobbies
Projects	Sports
Equipment	Societies
Training	Lectures
Specialist Skills	Languages
Diploma	Awards
Travel	Funds

Repeat the exercise for each two-year period up to the present.

'What is the point of this?' All of us can recall things we did that we remember with pride. The times when we did more than we were asked to, where we dealt with an emergency, grasped an opportunity, solved a problem. They may or may not have been noticed or rewarded. This is irrelevant now but demonstrates vividly our skills and capabilities then and our potential for problem solving in the future.

'Why two years?' As you progress, a two-year period will be the approximate time that you did a particular job. Having completed this memory exercise, check to see that you have not left any deed or accomplishment out. It is vital to you that all that you have done in your life, thus far, has been recorded. You are now ready to progress to Stage 2.

Before the Search Begins

ANALYSIS OF TRANSFERABLE SKILLS

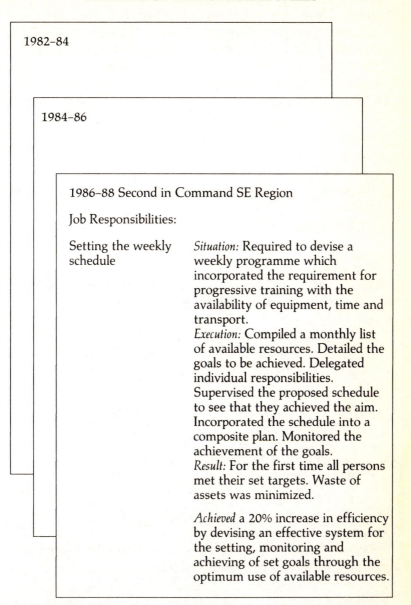

Figure 2 *Example of Analysis of Transferable Skills*

Stage 2
Examine each accomplishment in turn and pose the question 'So what?', then enter your answer in the next column, under the following headings:

Situation: What did you face that required your action?
Execution: What was your plan to deal with the situation?
Result: What was the result of your plan?

Stage 3
Now summarize each accomplishment into a short but complete statement, avoiding any words listed under A and incorporating one of the words shown as power words in Figure 3.

Stage 4
Examine each six-year time frame, mentally sort your accomplishments into the order that gave you the most satisfaction, then annotate them numerically in the right-hand column.

Examining the order you gave to your accomplishments should achieve two results:

1. A base guide to the type of challenges you enjoy and thrive at and thus an idea of the type of second career you wish to embark on.
2. A guide to what should be included in your CV (curriculum vitae).

Stage 5
Money is the key word which governs the actions of all business. You must therefore show a potential employer that by hiring you he can ultimately:

Make money – By increasing sales, developing markets, attracting new customers and retaining old customers; or

Before the Search Begins

A. Avoid   (These are wishy-washy words which degrade your accomplishment.)

Observed
Responsible for
Involved in
Part of
Ordered to, etc.

B. Use

Accomplished	Held	Revised
Achieved	Headed	Researched
Administered		Reallocated
Analysed	Implemented	Recruited
Approved	Increased	Retained
	Improvised	
Built	Installed	Solved
Budgeted	Inducted	Staffed
	Invented	Set up
Created	Improved	Simplified
Controlled		Sold
Conceived	Led	Streamlined
Converted	Launched	Strengthened
Conducted		Succeeded
Commanded	Managed	Supervised
	Maintained	Superseded
Developed	Motivated	
Directed	Moved	Trained
Doubled		Tripled
Demonstrated	Negotiated	Traced
Designed		Transformed
Devised	Organized	Trimmed
Delivered	Operated	Translated
	Originated	
Established		Unified
Earned	Produced	Unravelled
Eliminated	Planned	Uncovered
Expanded	Performed	Used
Evaluated	Promoted	
	Processed	Verified
Formed	Purchased	Validated
Formulated	Provided	
Froze	Presented	Withdrew
Founded		Withheld
Forecast	Reorganized	Worked
	Redesigned	Wrote
Generated	Reduced	Won
Grabbed	Recommended	

Figure 3 *Power Words for a CV*

Save money   – By increasing efficiency, better management or strategic planning, improved administration, streamlined distribution, cutting costs and improving productivity; or

Create money   – By using the skills that only you possess within the company.

The key to marketing yourself is to identify where your skills lie, support them with examples, and translate those skills into ones valued by an employer.

Compare these two extracts from a CV:

Example 1

1989–1991. Squadron Second-in-Command in Germany. Responsible to Company Commander for writing the Training Programme and supervising the office staff. Responsible for the 1990 NCO's Cadre. Unit baggage officer for 1991 annual training in Canada.

Example 2

1989–1991

- Executive Officer/Corporate Planner of 140-man unit in Germany with special responsibility for administration and the maintenance of 140 men and equipment valued at approximately £16 million.
- Devised and directed a career development and training course to improve efficiency and reduce wastage.
- Planned and implemented the successful move to Canada of 800 men and freight, requiring the allocation of manpower, distribution of freight and Just-in-Time logistic planning.

Example 2 reveals experience that a potential employer, not familiar with service life, can relate to and use. Example 1 does not.

Thus the final stage in this analysis of transferable skills is to re-read your notes and transpose your accomplishments into those skills which can be used by an employer.

Threat Analysis - Summing Up the Opposition

No good military appreciation can be made without a serious analysis of the enemy. During career transition, there are two enemies which require addressing.

The enemy within
However determined, prepared and confident one might feel at the commencement of this undertaking there will be self-doubts. Such doubts strike at the very foundation of your plan and undermine self-confidence. I have called these enemies the 'Waddaeyenos'. The enemy within can easily be defeated through positive thought, for example:

Waddaeyeno about sales?
You have been a salesman all your service career. All you need is a thorough understanding of the product, the ability to explain it and its use to others, and the self-confidence to demonstrate the benefits its use will bring to its users. Sounds like a service instructor?

Waddaeyeno about human resources?
What you do not know can be learned, for just as there are military regulations to provide guidance to the personnel manager in the Service, there are regulations which govern the HR functions in the corporate world. An advantage that you have is that you have probably been managing a limited number of people more thoroughly, with greater depth and with a deeper understanding of their personal problems and their aspirations, and planning their professional education and career paths than most HR professionals.

Waddaeyeno about management?
A great deal more than you might think. You have been

trained by, arguably, the finest management training organization in the country. You have been taught to listen to advice then form your decision. You have been taught the importance of meticulous and detailed planning. You have been practised in materiel management and the management of resources. You have been taught self-confidence. You have motivated others and provided leadership. You have been practised in solving problems. What else is management?

Waddaeyeno about business?
Really quite a lot. You have husbanded resources, taken calculated risks, persuaded others to 'buy' what you are selling, made things, produced things, distributed things, accounted for things, been competitive and have a determination to succeed. The only thing you have not done so far is do it for profit! Well, now you have a chance.

Got the idea?

The threat to the family unit
There are serious threats to the family during the job search. They are mostly brought about by a combination of fear of the unknown, changes in domestic routine and the threat to financial security. As explained earlier, it is vital that when you begin to make your strategic plan you make the plan together. Then there are no surprises which, in turn, should help to strengthen the family unit.

Preparation for Planning

Investment in equipment
A guide to preparing your CV is given in Chapter 4; however, it is as well to remember that your job search will not be easy and will require much dedication. You will be writing lots of letters, preparing many different CVs and keeping track of many different people – at the same time you will probably not have a secretary or clerk. You might

then consider buying the following equipment to support your task. The expenditure will prove worth while.

Computer/Word processor. This will allow you to tailor individual CVs, mail merge standard letters, check your spelling and keep track of your search. There are now a large number of second-hand quality machines on the market which could reduce the capital expense. There are also discount software firms which offer suitable word processing software at well below list price. Some small firms are springing up which lease computers; most deal with small businesses, but they are worth talking to and will give advice as to which machine suits your requirement best.

Printer. Vital for all the above reasons. It is equally important to ensure that your paperwork looks professional, therefore the printer must be near letter quality (NLQ).

Filing cabinet. You cannot keep your correspondence in shoe boxes!

Quality paper. A supply of top quality paper in white or ivory is recommended.

Index cards. I recommend that you keep a supply of 4" × 6" index cards for note-taking during interviews, research on target companies and for networking.

Answer-phone. These can now be purchased quite reasonably, and are vital. No one searching for a new job can afford to miss an important call whether it be from a potential employer, a networking contact or even a head hunter. It is a sad fact of modern business life that busy people who call and receive no answer may not bother to call again.

Establishing the routine

You are not starting a part-time hobby. You are embarking on the single most important task that you face at present.

The Job Assault Course

This search is a full-time occupation; so just as you prepared or used the weekly training programme, prepare your own programme. Figure 4 is one such example.

Inevitably, at some time you will be working from your home. Those changing careers from the Service are at a disadvantage. Not for us the use of the 'firm's' facilities or the out-placement services as provided by so many corporations. Therefore, there will be distractions: the sunny day, the wife and kids, the pet. The only way to minimize the temptations is to set up your office and keep office hours and the office routine.

Set up an office in a spare room or portion of a room. Equip it with the office tools listed on page 27 and a telephone or extension. Then make sure that everyone knows that when you are in your 'office' you are not to be disturbed.

Establish a weekly programme and keep a record of your progress. An example of a weekly programme is shown in Figure 4.

WEEKLY PROGRAMME

Monday	Results
Follow up phone calls Scan weekend ads Research target companies Send out marketing letters	
Tuesday	**Results**
Set up appointments Write target companies Find 3 new network contacts Interviews	
Wednesday	**Results**
Scan midweek ads Make missed phone calls Contact network Take exercise	
Thursday	**Results**
Attend meetings Answer ads Thank you notes Information phone calls	
Friday	**Results**
Follow up last week's actions Mail more marketing letters Review contact list Research on potential target companies	
Saturday/Sunday	**Results**
Social interviews Research next week's interviews Practise interview technique	

Figure 4 *Example of a Weekly Programme*

The Job Assault Course

CHAPTER 3
Creating the Framework

The Network

Everyone has heard about the Old Boy Network. It is, thank heavens, alive and kicking. It will become your most important and valuable tool in the search. This chapter will deal with how to create successfully your own large and ever-expanding network.

The Aim
The aim of creating a network is eventually to get an interview with a person who could hire you. (En route to these important people you will speak to others in your network who can be described as 'information givers'.)

The Rings of Confidence

Consider that there are three concentric rings that I have called the rings of confidence.

The ring of friends
The outer ring is made up of all those people who you know. Take a piece of paper and your address book, Christmas card list and visitors' book and write down everyone you know. Not necessarily close friends only, for if you have spent a substantial time in uniform inevitably they will be in a similar profession, and perhaps position, as yourself. Now add to that list all those with whom you come into

The Job Assault Course

professional contact, such as doctor, lawyer, bank manager, insurance man, vicar. Now consider adding those others with whom you have professional contacts: postman, plumber, electrician, garage owner, etc. What you are trying to create is a data bank from which you can elicit further contacts.

No, you are not likely to be offered a job by the plumber, but all these people are in daily contact with other businesses and in other offices with people who have information – information which you might want in the future.

With diligence you should have a list of over 60. Now start to divide that list into those who are likely to know someone in the type of position you are seeking, and those who might know someone in a company employing a person who does the type of job that you are seeking.

Enter these lists into your network file and be ready to contact them when you start the campaign.

The ring of informants
The next ring are those who you will wish to contact for information. Such information as:

1. Hiring contacts
2. Further network contacts
3. Information on a particular industry or company
4. Ideas on what type of company could use your skills.

The ring of informants will be made up from some of those who you already know, further contacts resulting from those you contact and contacts you find through professional organizations, such as:

1. Retired Officers/NCO Associations
2. Regimental Associations/Clubs
3. Rotary/Businessmen's Clubs and local social clubs holding lists of those members who are willing to help others in 'career transition'.

4. Professional bodies, such as professional associations, and universities.

The hiring ring
This is the goal, the ring of people who you want to meet. The people who can hire you or recommend that you be hired. Having done your research, having targeted your company, having asked all the questions, the people in this ring are those to whom you want to be introduced or recommended.

CHAPTER 4
Baiting the Hook: The Curriculum Vitae and Marketing Letter

Reason and Purpose of a CV

Ask any 100 knowledgeable people and you will find 99 experts on how a CV should be composed. Unfortunately, no two will agree.

The most important purpose of a CV is to whet the appetite of the reader, excite his interest and entice him to offer you an interview. Excite his interest; do not let him know all there is to know about you!

A CV is your personal advertisement. Like all the best advertisements it should cover the following:

- Capture the attention of the reader.
- Pique his/her interest.
- Extol the best features of the product (you).
- Tell the truth.
- Show why the product is needed.
- Tell why the reader cannot do without it.
- Be simple, clear and easily understood.

There are three different types of CV/Résumé. Each is aimed at a different audience. All three complement each other and assist your job search.

The general CV
This CV is for the consumption of your network 'ring of friends'. Its aim is to give them an idea of who you are, where your talents lie and how they can help you.

The information CV
This CV is refined and closely edited. It has probably been produced when you have a general understanding of those areas where you want to put your skills to work.

This CV is aimed at search firms and those who are professional CV readers like the internal recruiters of large firms and those who we have called the 'network information ring'. These CVs should conform to some basic principles. The reader will have received hundreds of CVs; he/she will have an attention span of no more than 30 seconds, therefore they are looking for an easy-to-read, clear, succinct, attractive paper.

The tailored CV
This is a stand-alone CV. It has been tailored to reflect the needs of a particular company or position either through your research or by analysis of a particular advertisement. It is used to answer advertisements or aimed at target companies/organizations. This type of CV is time consuming to construct but has proved effective.

How to compose your CV
In Chapter 2 your appreciation revealed your transferable skills – these we shall include under a general heading of DEMONSTRATED STRENGTHS.

The same exercise gave you a chronological order of what you have done so far. Using the exercise as a guide, list what you have done in reverse chronological order: start with what you are doing now and work backwards. Give this a general heading of SIGNIFICANT RESULTS.

Next, under a heading of EMPLOYMENT just list the job titles that you filled in, in reverse chronological order.

Under the heading EDUCATION list your academic history.

Using a heading entitled SPECIAL QUALIFICATIONS list other qualifications including:

Language qualifications
Membership of professional bodies

Useful service courses (ie useful to an employer)
Special awards
Publications – any relevant article published.

Finally, under a heading of INTERNATIONAL EXPERIENCE, list those countries that you have worked in and those in which you have travelled extensively.

Winnowing and translating

Winnowing
Now start the process of winnowing out the irrelevant, the obscure and the confusing. Ensure that what you have left is short, pithy and expressive, and in good English. Not too easy I can assure you.

Translating
It is worth repeating what we said earlier: *Money* is the key word which governs the actions of all business. You must therefore show a potential employer that by hiring you he can ultimately:

- Make money
- Save money
- Create money.

Now try to quantify what you did in numbers of workers, value of responsibility or savings in quantity, time or cash. For example:

A tank	=	£2 million.
An aircraft	=	£6 million.
Squadron group	=	approximately 200 workers. £40 million of equipment and stores.
A machine shop	=	£4 million in stores.

Using the power words (see Figure 3 on page 23) define exactly what your responsibilities were and translate your appointments into civilian terms.

Baiting the Hook: The Curriculum Vitae and Marketing Letter

You should now have your work history explained in terms that can be more readily understood by a potential employer who has only the sketchiest idea of the military. You also have the basis of all the different CVs that you might produce.

CV words of caution
A CV is not the only weapon in your arsenal. It is sometimes better to use it like a calling card, to confirm an impression or to give an interviewer something to talk about. So while the present subject is CVs they should be used in conjunction with marketing letters and personal contacts. Similarly, try to dissuade your friends from handing out your CVs too freely. You then lose contact with them and the result is that you cannot control your follow-up action.

There are a number of agencies who advertise that, for a fee, they will write your CV for you. The fact that they make a living out of providing this service testifies that they satisfy some customers. My comment is that no one knows you better than yourself. This is your personal marketing tool which you may wish to refine and adjust and which reflects your personality – would you allow others to write your love letters for you?

CV format
It is generally agreed that there are two different formats for a CV: the chronological and the functional.

The reverse chronological CV emphasizes *your employment record* – your job, your title, where you worked, for how long, and with what level of responsibility. As the name suggests it is listed in reverse chronological order.

The functional CV emphasizes what *kind of work you have done*, what results you achieved and in what different areas.

While without doubt the chronological CV is the most common and the one which recruiters most expect, the advantage of the functional format is that it de-emphasizes parts of your experience and highlights the more relevant skills and knowledge. The functional format groups work experience by business function such as Management, Special Projects, Finance. It also incorporates significant results which illustrate the level of experience in each field.

Remember that the CV is your personal marketing tool and therefore you should construct it so that it has the best chance of achieving your mission. Indeed, you may decide that a combination of the two different formats may serve you best.

Dressing the CV
The CV must be easy to read and must catch the eye; therefore try to incorporate the following dos and don'ts:

Do
- Leave plenty of 'white space' on your CV.
- Be positive but accurate.
- Include only enough to whet the reader's appetite.
- Keep sentences short.
- Dress up the paper using heavy type, capital letters and underlining words.

Don't
- Allow spelling mistakes or errors in grammar.
- Use the first person singular.
- Include salary requirements.
- Include references.
- Include jargon, abbreviations or slang.

The length of the CV will depend largely on the length of your experience and service. Although many will say that a CV should be one page, this is in fact only to help the professional CV reader. Provided that the guide lines given above are followed, there is no reason why a CV should not be two, three or even four pages long.

Preparing your CV
Following this chapter are two blank formats in different styles (Chronological CV, Figure 5 and Functional CV,

CHRONOLOGICAL CV

(Name)
(Address)
(City, County, Postcode)
(Telephone No)

BACKGROUND SUMMARY OF SKILLS

WORK EXPERIENCE

Location
Dates
Job title and scope of responsibilities
   Accomplishments:
   -
   -
   -

Location
Dates
Job title and scope of responsibilities
   Accomplishments:
   -
   -
   -

EDUCATION

School
University/Higher education
Degree(s)

SPECIAL QUALIFICATIONS AND LANGUAGES
(optional)

PERSONAL
(optional)

Figure 5 *Example of a Chronological CV*

FUNCTIONAL CV

(Name)
(Address)
(City, County, Postcode)
(Telephone No)

BACKGROUND SUMMARY OF SKILLS

MAJOR ACCOMPLISHMENTS
(by function)

-
-
-
-
-
-
-
-

WORK EXPERIENCE

Employer
Location
Dates
Job title and scope of responsibilities

EDUCATION

School
University/Higher education
Degree(s)

SPECIAL QUALIFICATIONS AND LANGUAGES
(optional)

PERSONAL
(optional)

Figure 6 *Example of a Functional CV*

Figure 6). Try filling in each one, eventually finding a format that suits you best.

Pull together your first attempt and get it constructively criticized by someone else.

When you have a CV that you feel is your marketing tool it is time to decide how to print it. Whatever method you choose, it must look professional. There are a number of alternatives:

- Produce and print your own on your PC.
- Hire a word processor.
- Hire a typing firm.
- Take a copy to a printers.

Ideally, you should retain a copy on a disk so that you can produce additional copies.

The Marketing Letter

Reason and purpose of the marketing letter

A marketing letter is just that, a letter sent to a potential employer which markets you (the product). It is used as one of your marketing tools and can replace the CV. Note, as we mentioned earlier, that if possible you should try to avoid sending out your CV unless one is demanded.

Chapter 5 will cover how to make a marketing plan, but you will find that the largest job market is the so-called hidden market. Your research and networking contacts will lead you to some and the marketing letter will reveal others.

In essence, the marketing letter, used in conjunction with a marketing plan, is a letter aimed at employers who do not have jobs advertised but whom you, through your research, think could use your expertise. In other words, your letter piques the interest, and strikes a chord in an employer's mind so that he gives you an interview. The types of situation where a marketing letter could be used include situations such as:

1. You have targeted a promising company but you cannot reach, or perhaps identify, the decision maker. You marketing letter, addressed to a high-level executive, may get his/her attention or be passed to the correct person.
2. You have identified the right person but cannot contact him on the telephone. You tell the secretary that you are writing and ask him/her to bring it to the executive's attention.
3. In addition to your target companies you have uncovered some other promising prospects but you cannot give them your total attention immediately. You address a carefully tailored letter to the Managing Director and send the letters out at a steady rate (so that you keep track for follow-up).

Types of marketing letters

During your campaign each letter you write can be called a marketing letter. Listed below are some of the major types:

1. **The Broadcast Letter.** Addressed to a number of potential target companies, it tells your story without a CV.
2. **The Search Letter.** This is addressed to executive search firms. It normally consists of your CV with a covering letter which summarizes your background, what position you are looking for and an indication of the salary bracket you seek.
3. **The Advert Reply Letter** in response to an advertisement. It comprises two parts: a prologue which shows how you fit the principal specifications for the job, added to a standardized body of the letter drawn from your broadcast letter.
4. **The Tailor-made Letter.** Aimed at a specific individual within a specific company, it is often designed to stand on its own without a CV. It is like a rifle rather than a machine gun.

Baiting the Hook: The Curriculum Vitae and Marketing Letter

5. **The Follow-up Letter.** An informal letter, possibly hand written, to cover thank yous, agree the next step or act as a reminder.

Guidelines for a marketing letter
1. Keep in mind what your target wants:

   Increased Sales

   Decreased Expenses

   } Thus you have to sell your accomplishments and special skills to illustrate how you could match the targets.

2. Sell your accomplishments and show the relevance of your experience.
3. Keep to current experiences.
4. Observe two-page limit.
5. Leave out:

   Dates
   Personal details
   Salary discussion
   References
   CV.

6. End up with a very polished letter.

The opening paragraph
The opening paragraph must grab the executive's attention with something that answers one of his/her needs, not one of your needs.

It will probably be one of your accomplishments and may be dressed up in one or other of the following 'attention getters':

- *Addressing Needs.* This approach highlights a problem, common to the industry, revealed through your research, and suggests how you might solve it.

- *The Story*. In this method you talk about something, very interesting and relevant, that you have done, such as your South American tour with the Defence Sales Team.
- *The Current Event*. This is where you relate your experience to something that is being widely discussed within the industry.
- *The Direct Method* is where you open with who you are, what you have done and what you want. It is not the recommended approach for those changing careers!

Subsequent paragraphs
Having grabbed the attention with the opening paragraph you now weave into the letter paragraphs which cover the following:

- Major achievements – quantified if possible.
- Challenges and how you solved them.
- Skills and experience.

Not too many or in too much detail – leave something for the interview.

The closing paragraph
The closing paragraph can be divided in three:

Why you have singled out the company. Everyone likes to hear nice things about their company and this is a chance to say it, but too much sounds sarcastic! The real reason you chose the company is through research and because it fits what you want.

What you want from the company – the hidden job.

Baiting the Hook: The Curriculum Vitae and Marketing Letter

How are you going to follow up. Suggested endings include:

> 'My wide experience and skills are only covered briefly in this letter. I would appreciate the opportunity to discuss with you how this experience could benefit your company.
>
> I will phone your office next week to arrange an appointment.
>
> Yours sincerely'

> 'The expansion of ACME's operations into Europe presents the type of exciting challenge that I am looking for and I would welcome the chance to explore how my expertise could match your needs.
>
> I look forward to hearing from your office.
>
> Yours sincerely'

> 'ACME is recognized as a leader in applying total quality control. Your recent acquisition of Gridiron Industries presents a challenge which, as an experienced logistics manager, I am qualified to meet.
>
> It would be pleasant to exchange ideas and to hear from you what you think the next five years hold for ACME.
>
> Yours sincerely'

The Job Assault Course

Rehearsing at home

CHAPTER 5
Putting the Plan into Operation

The Execution of the Plan

By now you have prepared your plan in individual parts. Next you must incorporate the parts into an overall operational strategy. In military terms what has been covered thus far in this book are the headings:

GROUND
SITUATION – own forces and opposition
MISSION

What we are now going to cover is the EXECUTION.

Like any military operation, landing the right job is achieved by progressing through a number of phases. Some phases may happen simultaneously, some phases may be skipped owing to favourable conditions and at times the plan may have to move back a phase.

There are five phases:

Phase 1: The gathering of information to identify likely targets and potential allies.
Phase 2: The use of contacts and marketing resources to arouse interest.
Phase 3: The skirmish and initial engagement.
Phase 4: The set piece engagement.
Phase 5: The offer and the terms of the treaty.

The Job Assault Course

The first three phases are outlined in this chapter and suggestions or advice are included.

Phase 4 – the set piece engagement – refers to job interviews, while Phase 5 is about negotiation and evaluation of a job offer. Separate chapters are devoted to interviewing techniques and job offers.

Where the Jobs Are

Before embarking on your job campaign it is worth understanding where jobs are to be found. Statistics indicate that jobs are found as follows:

Advertisements 10%	Advertised jobs include both 'open' – those that have the name of the company listed – and 'blind' – those that only have a box number for replies. Answering both types will be discussed later.
Recruitment Agencies and Search Firms 7%	
Unadvertised or Hidden Jobs 83%	Such jobs include those that are recruited by word of mouth, those that are passed to you by contacts, those that only the employer knows about – the retirement, promotion or sacking of the present incumbent – and the jobs that you create by identifying a need and persuading an employer to create a job for you.

Thus if the statistics are correct *eight out of every ten jobs are not advertised* and are not known to recruiters. While not forgetting or ignoring advertisements or recruiters, the most time should be devoted to finding the hidden jobs.

Phase 1: Intelligence gathering

The temptation might be immediately to start visiting all those in your network, distribute your CV on a wide scale, state what your objective is and then ask the networker to suggest what jobs you might be able to do. Well, everyone likes to be able to help and they probably will, but you are asking strangers, who do not know you well, to judge what you are capable of, when you know yourself the best. You are squandering an asset.

First, think of all the types of companies that use your expertise. Let us say that your prime skill is in logistics, that is, in moving and supplying or, in business terms, distribution. Who is in the business of distribution? Suppliers of raw material to industry, suppliers of finished products to wholesalers and retailers, freight movers, freight forwarders and distribution companies among many others.

Second, visit your local library and Chamber of Commerce, research the advertising lists, Yellow Pages and business directories, and list those companies, in your chosen area, who engage in your special area of expertise. You now have the basis of a *target list*. Divide this list into those companies that your network might be able to introduce you to and those companies which, because of geography, you will include in a marketing plan.

Third, using the resources of your library, find out as much as you can about your target companies. Many libraries now have on computer, microfilm or microfiche the annual reports of companies who trade on the Stock Exchange; they may also have extracts of articles written in newspapers and periodicals about your target companies. Such articles may include the names of rival companies which can be added to your target list.

Fourth, research the material you have gathered and consult the different company directories until you have found the names of key executives within the target companies.

Fifth, return to the library and, using the *Yearbook of Recruitment and Employment Services*, research and compile a list of recruiting firms which are generalists or which specialize in your field. Again, divide them into those to which your network might effect an introduction and those that should be included in your marketing plan. Again, annotate the names of the recruiters who work for the firms.

Sixth, if your target company list includes public quoted companies (ones trading on the Stock Exchange) telephone the company and ask for the Investor Relations Department or PR Department. Identify yourself as someone who is interested in investing in the company – no lie, you are thinking of investing yourself – and request a copy of their Annual Report and any subsequent financial reports. If the company is not publicly quoted, telephone or visit the Sales Department and request brochures/leaflets on the company's products or services. This information will prove worth while when preparing your marketing letters and preparing for an interview.

You are now in a position to prepare a task schedule, activate your network and commence your marketing plan.

Phase 2: Use of contacts and marketing resources

Activating your network
Start by placing a telephone call to each of your network. Remind them of who you are, what you are seeking and why you believe they may be of assistance. Then set up meetings, convenient to them, of no more than *half an hour* each. It is reasonable to assume that they are busy people and that you should be able to discuss what you want within that period. It also enables them to fit you into their daily schedules. Take care only to take on a balanced number of meetings each week. Do not forget that you will be carrying out other activities as well. Networking is a two-way street. Your aim is to gather information, increase your contacts

Putting the Plan into Operation

ACTION PLAN FOR A NETWORK INTERVIEW

Networking visit to: **On:**

Address: **Time:**

INTRODUCTION: Small talk to break the ice/catch up on old times

YOUR BACKGROUND AND SKILLS   2 mins

WHAT YOU ARE LOOKING FOR   2 mins

RESEARCH AND TARGETS   6 mins

INFORMATION YOU CAN GIVE

NOTES

FOLLOW-UP ACTION

SECRETARY'S NAME   *FILE REF:*

Figure 7 *Action Plan for a Network Interview*

and to effect an introduction to those who may be seeking to hire someone like you.

In turn, your network is hoping to increase their network (when you find the position you seek you may be a valuable asset), gather information (you may already have insight or information that may be of help) and store up goodwill, either with you or through introducing you to your future employer.

It is important, therefore, that when you have secured your meeting you prepare an individually tailored visit plan aimed at the effective management of your time together. The group headings are given in Figure 7. This plan should, if possible, include time to find out areas where you can be of help to your network partner either through your experience, your research or, perhaps, contacts from within your network. When preparing your visit plan consider the following:

1. Can I encapsulate my background and skills inside two minutes?
2. Can I state what type of job I am looking for inside two minutes?
3. Can I say what information I am looking for, companies I have researched, contacts I am seeking, suggestions I would appreciate and other people whom I should meet inside six minutes?
4. What do I know about the business that my contact is engaged in? Do I know of any general problems afflicting that industry?
5. Is there anything that I have uncovered during my research that might interest my contact professionally?

The answers to the questions will help to fill in the visit action plan. Note that the time that has been devoted to your talking is limited to approximately ten minutes. The remaining time is devoted to your listening, following up suggestions, offering ideas and contributing to the networking visit.

Putting the Plan into Operation

Do not overstay your allotted time. At the end of the 30 minutes gather up your information, agree any follow-up action with contacts, that is, establish who is going to follow up first, whether you can use a person's name, whether you should write or telephone first, etc. Hand over a copy of your CV, thank them for their time, promise to keep them informed of your progress, and leave.

Follow-up action
As soon as possible send a thank you letter.

Enter into your files all the information, advice, suggestions and contacts that you gleaned from the meeting.

Annotate what follow-up action was decided. Note who was going to initiate the first contact with new additions to your network, and enter into your work diary when the contact will be made and when you should telephone to try to set up a meeting.

Update your network list.

Marketing/Broadcast letter to target companies

In Chapter 4 marketing letters and target CVs were discussed; during this phase in your job search campaign you start to send out your carefully tailored marketing letter.

Review your list of target companies and select those into which you are unable to network, perhaps because of their geographical location. Examine the information that you have gathered about those companies and about the industry in general. From this information try to identify the following:

1. *The name of an executive officer in the company to whom you can address your letter.* Do not necessarily select the Chairman or Managing Director; look for the person who may be your boss, ie if you are seeking a job in sales, target the Sales Director.
2. *Problems that are identified, or hinted at, in the Annual Report.*

Remember that the Annual Report is a public relations/advertising brochure for the investor. It is not likely to reveal detailed problems unless they have been resolved. Carefully worded indications in the Chairman's address or figures in the financial report will usually indicate problem areas if read closely. For example, mention of improvements to customer services are often covers for problems with distribution or with after-sales service. 'Reduction in profits owing to an unexpected downturn in customer demands' is a euphemism for marketing problems or a loss of a major contract.

3. *Problems facing the industry as a whole.* Reading the financial press and trade magazines will identify some of the major common problems; however, your best source of information is from your network.
4. *Latest trends in that industry.* Again, your best source of information lies within your network.
5. *Acquisitions or expansions made by the target company.* Information can be gathered through reading the company report, the financial press and through your contacts. What you are trying to uncover are yet unannounced job openings. For example, 'Opening of new markets' means that someone has to handle them. 'Streamlining a new acquisition' means sacking some of the old management and the probable hiring of replacements.

Identify which of your skills backed by experience are most relevant to the target company. Which skills might solve a problem you have uncovered, exploit a potential job opening or replace the skills of someone who has been promoted or resigned?

Armed with the information you have gathered and using the guide lines given in Chapter 4, craft your marketing letter. Proof read it to verify that it might arouse curiosity or excite interest and then address it to the executive in person.

Initially, the marketing letter will be time consuming but

the preparation time will speed up and a word processor will enable you to incorporate relevant paragraphs from other letters.

Control the release of your marketing letters; remember that you will have to follow up each one and it is estimated that on average it requires three telephone calls to get in touch with a specific individual. If you send out 30 letters to target companies, the following week you might have to make up to 90 telephone calls and spend as much as four hours on the phone.

30 letters = 60 unsuccessful 2-minute telephone calls
= 120 min
30 successful 4-minute telephone calls
= 120 min
240 minutes on telephone = 4 hours

Recruitment agencies and search firms

Your research will have revealed the names of search firms and a contact in the firm. It is to be hoped that your network will effect a personal introduction to a recruitment agency in your area.

If you have been in uniform for most of your working life it is unlikely that you will have come into contact with search firms or, as they are unflatteringly nicknamed, 'head hunters'.

Search firms are organizations which make their money by recruiting personnel on assignment to fill specific job vacancies. The size of such organizations varies enormously from the top five with affiliated national and world-wide offices to local companies with one or two head hunters.

They are divided into two types: *retained*, who as the name suggests are retained by a number of organizations to fill key manning posts, and *contingency firms* who seek out organizations with manning requirements and then find potential candidates. Occasionally they seek out candidates then offer them to potential clients.

Both types are usually paid, less a retainer, only when a

candidate is hired, normally with a percentage of the annual salary of the successful candidate. Owing to the high overheads associated with a search and the exhaustive background checks and interviews, search firms normally only fill the higher paid positions. There is a third type of firm which requires a finder's fee from the job seeker. At times, they represent themselves as search firms but they are closer to employment agencies and offer no guarantee for your money of finding the type of job you seek. There have been stories of such firms setting up interviews for jobs for which candidates are wholly unsuited, thus wasting time, money and lowering morale. Candidates reading this book should never need to pay anyone before landing a job. Employment agencies may not, by law, take fees from job seekers.

Retained and contingency search firms depend upon their reputations and thus can be trusted. Neither type of firm is working for you, only for its client. Thus, unless you match closely the requirements of the search at present under way you are unlikely to be considered. Most firms receive hundreds of unsolicited CVs, especially in the present economic climate. Usually, such CVs are quickly read and if they do not match a current search are filed and retained for four to six months.

Do not assume that your CV will be passed on to other offices of the same firm. Send each office a copy.

Statistically, search firms fill less than 10 per cent of the job market. Their searches are constrained by the job specifications drawn up by their clients. You will perhaps appreciate that those who are changing careers are less likely to find a new job this way. Do not, however, discard this source. Who knows what their next client requires? It may be someone with exactly the same skills you possess.

Marketing letter to a search firm
This type of letter was discussed in Chapter 4. Draft a covering letter to the individual whose name you uncovered during your research.

Putting the Plan into Operation

Blind advertisement

GENERAL MANAGER – HEAD OF OPERATIONS

60-year-old multi-faceted transportation and distribution company is seeking an experienced General Manager – Head of Operations.

Successful candidate must be able to manage headquarter and satellite operations effectively while providing the vision to propel dynamic organization into the 21st century.

Successful candidate must possess demonstrated:

- Hands-on operational, financial and organizational skills.
- Strong judgement and decision-making skills.
- Ability to develop and implement productivity and quality improvements.

Candidates must have ten years of key management experience in a £7–10 million service-related business. MBA or similar desirable. Attractive compensation package.

Send CV and covering letter to:

Box 9870 Daily Diatribe, W23 4BD

Open advertisement

GENERAL MANAGER

SMALL BUT GROWING manufacturer of power supply products with ten-year track record of innovation and market leadership in its sector of business. Turnover last year approached £2 million.

Founders are now looking for a person with the leadership and management skills to join as Chief Executive/General Manager to consolidate its international expansion and lead the company through its next phase of growth.

If you are that person, for more details please contact

John Prester, POWER SUPPLY plc, 3 Hightek Road, Ravenburgh RX2 5LE. Tel 0123 456789

Figure 8 *Examples of Blind and Open Advertisements*

The letter should be succinct and cover the following:

- Type of position you are seeking.
- Type of company/industry and geographical area.
- Renumeration range.
- You should enclose your CV.

Answering advertisements
As mentioned earlier there are two types of job advert listed in the press: examples of each are given in Figure 8.

The blind advert
These adverts give a description of the position which allows the job seeker to match skills against requirement, but such adverts do not include the name of the company, a contact or a telephone number, or its location, merely a box number. This makes research impossible.

There are a number of reasons why such adverts are placed. They include:

- A trawl to find out the quality of those in the job market.
- Employment agencies filling their pools of potential candidates. In the present economic climate, this is now most unlikely.
- Suspicious companies checking on the loyalty of their employees.
- Companies checking to see if a candidate has information on a rival.

All the reasons shown above have been used at some time, but by far and away the main reason is that there are so many responses to all adverts that the anonymity of a box number allows the company/agent to screen applicants without having to reply to or acknowledge applications. Nor do they have to answer the questions of unqualified job seekers.

Trade journals do not divulge the box number addressee, but if a Post Office box is used, and provided it has been reserved by a company rather than an individual, it may be possible to telephone the local Post Office where the box is located, and find out the name of the company. You will then have a starting point to begin your research. Answering blind advertisements is time consuming and not very productive and it is suggested that, unless the job sounds tailor-made for you, this activity be relegated to the very bottom of your work programme.

The open advert
These adverts appear in the press with a location, company name and a person or appointment to whom replies should be addressed. Remember that such jobs will still elicit hundreds of replies. Open advertisements do represent real jobs and thus are worth a reply but, in view of the poor return (one answer in twenty is a good average), do not spend too much time on your reply. Remember, only 17 per cent of jobs are filled through adverts.

To give yourself an advantage concentrate only on open ads and take the following steps which should give more attention to your reply than many others.

Cover letter for advertisements

- If you know the company but not the name of the person who will review your application, telephone and ask for the name of the head of personnel. Address your letter to that person. At least it will demonstrate your initiative.
- Telephone the company and try to find out the name of the head of the department to which this job will report and send him/her a copy as well. This manager is likely to receive fewer applications; thus yours, if well crafted, may pique the interest of the reader and lead to an interview.
- Research the company's Annual Report to find the name of an individual to whom to write.
- Cover letters should contain three topics:
  – What attracts you to the company

- Why the company should be attracted to you
- Your desire to meet for discussion.

Start by making your letter original. Replace 'Reference your advertisement 16th August' with a company policy, programme or achievement that you admire which you have found through research. This may hold the reader's attention and demonstrate your resourcefulness.

The second paragraph should consist of a few short sentences that demonstrate just how your experience matches the requirements for the position.

When concluding the letter, avoid giving away the initiative. Take responsibility for the follow-up by writing that you will telephone next week to arrange an appointment. Follow up as you promised for it shows genuine interest and does impress. If you are not going to get an interview anyway, it is much better to know early so that you can move on to something new.

Letter enclosure
Sending your all-purpose CV is like committing job-hunting suicide. If you have taken the time to reply to this advert, take the extra step and craft the enclosure as carefully as you did with the cover letter; it will be noticed.

Review your qualifications summary and make it specific to the job.

Begin by stating which job you are applying for:

Director International Distribution for ACME plc

Lay out your PERSONAL QUALIFICATIONS in such a way as to build a case for further investigation.

- 12 years' management experience in international freight movement.
- Extensive understanding of global distribution methods,

export regulations and air/land/sea cross loading operations.
- International background and global work experience.
- Skilled team builder both within an organization and with outside agencies.
- Willing to relocate overseas.

Support your summary with specific accomplishments which echo what the employer seeks in an 'Experience' section. Pack the best ammunition as early as possible in this CV.

The Human Resource Trap

If at all possible try to avoid falling into the HR trap; that is, being screened by the Personnel Department.

Human Resource Departments/Personnel Departments have a poor name among job seekers. In the majority of cases, this is not deserved for they are staffed by hard-working, experienced professionals.

This department is responsible for the demise of many applications by qualified, experienced candidates who are often the best choice for the position. It is worth understanding why this failure occurs:

- *An imprecise or too tight job specification.* Personnel Departments are often asked to draw up the specification for a new job. The manager will provide a list of job requirements but since this is a new position it has not been tested. The specification may include qualities and experience which have not been defined into categories of essential and desirable; thus many candidates are screened out.
- *The cult of the CV.* A cult has grown up that is subscribed to by many HR professionals. It is that future performance can only be judged by past experience, ie if you haven't done the same job somewhere else you can't do that job in the future; therefore, you should be screened

out. Anyone can see that this is ridiculous for the knack is to screen in people for a job rather than to screen them out. Yet it makes things easier for some who work in Personnel and saves them taking any chances.
- *HR is the last to know.* It is a sad fact that Personnel are frequently the last to know what is going on. Decisions to fire managers, open up new territories, buy new companies, expand operations and diversify responsibilities are often decided without consultation with HR. Thus they are not in a position to anticipate future hiring requirements.
- *Protect my job, protect my boss.* A policy of protectionism and isolationism can tend to obscure the true function of some personnel professionals. No one likes to make a mistake in front of the boss. Wasting his valuable time could be judged a mistake. So it is safer to weed out a candidate rather than recommend him/her for an interview. Similarly, some specialists delegate the initial screening of applications to junior members of the department who are less experienced and even less likely to show initiative and take a chance.

Human Resource professionals are servants of the management. At their best, they are committed to their company and are alert to anyone who may contribute to the well-being and success of the corporation. At worst, they are left out of the management loop, unwilling to make decisions and seeking ways to make their tasks easier. If at all possible, those in job transition should try to find another way into the company of their choice.

Follow-up action for Phase 2

- Expand your network and set up more network meetings.
- Research new companies that your networking has uncovered.

- Research the company of those people you are going to meet.
- Follow up marketing letters.
- Research interesting advertisements.
- Find contacts in target companies.
- Control release of marketing letters.
- Arrange informational interviews with network contacts.
- Continue Phase 1 operations.

Phase 3: The skirmish and initial engagement

This important phase of your operation is when you have been called for a first interview or have succeeded in networking yourself to a meeting with someone who could be a 'hirer'. In the case of a job interview, it will be your first exposure to two imprecise skills, ie interviewing and being interviewed.

The first interview – the interviewer
You will be faced by one of two types of interviewer:

The professional interviewer. This is likely to be a person in the Human Resource/Personnel Department or a manager who has attended a course of instruction on interview techniques. This type of interview is likely to be well constructed, succinct and tailored to the job opening. It is also likely to be rather impersonal and include one or two carefully crafted difficult questions. It is not likely to be very long as it is used to produce a list of potential candidates.

The amateur interviewer. Most people in management positions are amateurs when interviewing. This does not mean that the experience for the interviewee is any easier. You have to put the interviewer at his/her ease and he/she can ask difficult questions. The advantage lies in the fact that you can usually put across your personality more easily and you are likely to learn more about the company, if not the job in question.

Remember that in reaching this stage you have made a significant advance in your campaign; you could be near victory. At worst, this is the moment when all your previous hard work will be tested and it will serve as a rehearsal.

Remember the military saying, 'The first engagement is not the winning of the campaign'.

This is not the time to become complacent. All you have done is close with your target. Now is the time to increase your research, develop a specific plan, hone your personal skills and concentrate on winning this skirmish so that you will be invited back for the set piece engagement.

Detailed suggestions on preparing for and handling the different types of interview are laid out in Chapter 9.

Subsequent actions
Whether or not this interview is the prelude to further meetings, do not abandon your campaign plan. You may not be offered a job; equally you may not want to accept this job even if you were offered it. Do not lose momentum; continue to conduct your operation as follows:

- Send a thank you letter as demonstrated in Chapter 6.
- Make appointments with more network contacts.
- Continue your marketing and target letter plan.
- Follow up all leads.
- Continue research.
- Continue Phase 2 operations.

Phase 4: The set piece engagement

Subsequent interviews. This phase occurs when you are invited back for subsequent interviews for the job that you desire. I have used a military analogy so far when discussing the subsequent phases in your campaign to find a job. While the analogy still holds for much of this phase, the big difference is that this engagement is not adversarial. It is not you against them or a triumph of your will. Instead, you are both on the same side.

Putting the Plan into Operation

- The interviewer wants the best for the company and he/she thinks you are among the best.
- The interviewer is predisposed towards you. Who wants to keep on interviewing people?
- The interviewer wants you to admire his/her company and share in the enthusiasm for the job.
- The interviewee knows much more about the company and the job on offer as a result of the preliminary interview.
- The interviewee wants the job, is excited by the prospect and should be able to communicate his/her enthusiasm.
- The adrenaline is pumping on both sides; both are hoping for a successful conclusion.
- Both sides think that the candidate can do the job. It is now down to personalities and who is going to get on best with the other.

Your success in this crucial phase is dependent on three things and three things only:

- Research and preparation for the interview.
- Performance on the day.
- A pinch of luck.

While luck must rest with the gods, the other factors rest only with you and good preparation; a good performance will create its own good luck.

There are guide lines on the preparation and conduct of this phase of your campaign in Chapter 9.

Defeat at the engagement
If you do not progress to the final objective, do not allow yourself to become dejected or downhearted. To continue the military analogy, 'Withdraw, regroup, rearm, gather new intelligence and start to close with the enemy again'. In other words, return to Phase 2. Remember, if you have been conducting your job-search campaign as outlined you will already have prospects lined up and probably be

conducting preliminary interviews with at least one other good prospect; you may already have been called forward for a second interview. So learn from your experience:

- *Withdraw.* Send a thank you letter to the person who interviewed you expressing thanks for his/her time and renewed enthusiasm for the job.
- *Regroup.* Carry out a self-analysis as outlined in Chapter 9 and identify where things went wrong and how, if given another opportunity, you would improve.
- *Rearm.* Were there any areas where you showed that you were less knowledgeable perhaps than another candidate? If so, take time to update yourself either by reading up on the subject or by arranging an informational interview with a network partner.
- *Gather new intelligence.* Throw yourself into research about your next targets; update, refine and uncover more information.
- *Close with the enemy.* Continue trying to network into target companies and step up your marketing plan.

A different time-frame
In order to avoid frustration and disillusionment, it is important to realize that you and the targets of your job-search campaign are operating in a different time-frame.

You want to see immediate results for your hard effort. You want quick responses to your letters, your telephone calls returned, to be notified that your applications have been received, and speedy invitations to interviews.

Unfortunately, your job search is not foremost on the minds of those with whom you are communicating. Letters are answered only after the challenges of work have been satisfied. If pressure of work is intense your telephone call will be postponed. The HR Department will want to sift through all the job applicants before starting interviews. (In some cases this has taken months.) People are on seminars, sales trips, buying trips, inspections, out of town or even on holiday.

Putting the Plan into Operation

Your search will not progress at a smooth pace. It will have periods of intense activity interspaced with periods of inaction. This is why a multi-level approach is suggested and why an efficient filing system and follow-up programme are so important in order to keep track of your campaign.

Summary

Your job-search campaign should be a multi-level operation conducted over five phases. Your initial objective is to secure meetings. Meetings should then lead to initial interviews which in turn lead to subsequent interviews and finally to a job offer. Progress will not necessarily be a logical progression; there will be set-backs. Remember, your next meeting could be the one!

'You can't hang around the kennel – you have to go out and find some leads.'

CHAPTER 6
Keeping Track of Your Job Search Campaign

Files

In Chapter 2 preparing a filing system was mentioned. It is suggested that a minimum of three filing systems are maintained. Having said that, no filing system is of any use to any individual unless it is:

Comfortable: You are comfortable with the system that you adopt.
Workable: The system meets your needs and is easy to use.
Maintainable: You are able to update and maintain the information which the files contain.

Main file

This is where letters you receive and copies of letters you send out are kept; where the results of your research and information on companies are stored; where the results of your campaign are placed and where your private papers and financial information are filed. The most suitable filing system is probably old-fashioned drawer files locked in a filing cabinet.

The type of information you will have to record includes:

Marketing letters require:
A copy of the letter annotated with where to find the reference/research/background material.

Keeping Track of Your Job Search Campaign

A note of the name, address and telephone number of the recipient and the date you sent the letter.
A time-frame when you must follow up.
A record of the dates you telephoned – connected, tried, gave up and a record of the end result; thanks but no thanks, referred to someone else, secured appointment.
A record of any written reply you received.
A file note of what you decided to do.

Targeted letters require:
A copy of the letter with appropriate notes detailing what happened.

Answers to ads require:
The letter – the ad – the publication and date.
The results of research/telephone calls, etc.

Composite files

You will need to store examples of the different CVs and covering letters you have prepared; a list of your network and their telephone numbers and a one-page list of the leads that you are following up. In other words, these are files that you will be using to create new letters or files that you will be constantly updating.

Such information can, of course, be recorded in other filing systems such as address books, Rotadex phone books and in the filing cabinet. However, if you are using a computer with a word processing function you may find that storing this type of information on disk is the easiest way to retrieve, alter and maintain such information.

Network Cards

You have just returned to the house and the telephone rings. When you answer, the call is from a stranger whom you heard about at a network interview you had three weeks ago. You can remember nothing about the caller or why your contact said he/she might be of help. Or you are

NETWORK FILE CARD

Thomas J McDermott, VP Operations, The Company, 93 Valley Road, Chestertown, Lancs CH8 6LD. Tel: 0735 4900.

Meeting; 28 Jul – Introduced by Tom Folly see card No 187.
  Hiring freeze at The Company until end of Aug. The Company is expanding its Northampton Plant – Possible position in Sales, operations?

Contacts:
  Mr Henry Irvine, MD Parkinson Intl, Tel: 0876 4111.
    May be seeking an operations manager.
  Ms Angela Dubois, HR Director for Tanix Corp–May have some suggestions – McD will write letter of intro.
  James Lee, Partner in Mannix, Lee & Altway, Search firm. Use McD's name.

Future meetings: To be confirmed

CARD REFERENCE: 212

Figure 9 *Example of a Network File Card*

expecting a call and at last the telephone rings. This is no time to open the filing cabinet and rummage through files or to boot up the computer. This is the time to retrieve your network card file which you keep by the phone.

Network card files are 4" × 6" cards (or similar) on which you have recorded all the information you have gathered from a network meeting including possible future contacts. This card can be taken with you for subsequent meetings with your initial contact and can form warm-up interview material when you meet a subsequent contact.

An example of a network card file is shown in Figure 9.

Thank You Letters

Apart from being polite, courteous and good mannered, a thank you letter is an important support part of your job search, for the following reasons:

- It gives you a chance to include or emphasize qualifications which may not have emerged during the meeting.
- It provides an informal agenda for further action.
- The front runner for a job which you are after may withdraw and your expression of enthusiasm and reinforcement of your qualifications may be the factor which brings you forward once again.

There can be no hard and fast rule as to whether your letter should be handwritten or typed. It depends upon the neatness of your writing, who you are writing to and the reason for the meeting. It is worth noting that if you type any letter, type in the person's name, ie 'Dear Anne' or 'Dear Mr Black'. If you write the salutation in ink some people will think that the letter is a form letter sent to many people.

Thank you letters should always be written on good quality, plain paper. If the meeting has been between friends, as in a networking meeting, and your handwriting is neat and clear, your thank you letter should be written. Business letters and follow-ups to interviews can be typed. You are showing that you are a professional ready to enter the corporate world; note that most follow-up thank you letters from a company are typed and follow that example.

The Job Assault Course

CHAPTER 7
Preparing for and Conducting the Interview

Every meeting during your job search should be considered an interview. You are trying to sell yourself and create a favourable impression which will set you apart from other candidates. You want the person with whom you are meeting to remember you and if subsequently there is a situation which fits your experience, you want your name to spring to mind.

You never know where such an opportunity will come from. Therefore, every aspect should be anticipated, prepared for and rehearsed.

Following Up Your Letters by Telephone

Results from your mailing will be increased if you follow up with a telephone call.

Telephoning complete strangers – so called 'cold calling' – takes some getting used to. Until you have made sufficient calls to get over any feeling of discomfort it is suggested that you write down what you want to say. Of course, the content will vary depending on whether you are following up a network lead, a marketing letter or an advert. The basic headings will be:

- Who you are.
- Why you are calling – Mr/Ms Alpha suggested that I contact you – I wrote to you on the 15th and outlined my . . . I am following up your . . ., etc.

- What you want – A meeting.
- Your 60-second personal advertisement.

You should then rehearse so that it does not sound like a script.

You should prepare two further dialogues: one to deal with the secretary – see below – and one to leave on an answering machine. Only leave a message on a machine if you are desperate because you are not making contact.

The best time to follow up is one or two days after your letter has arrived, before it has been disposed of or forgotten. Ten days is too long.

Getting Past the Secretary

Your first contact with your target will probably be with his/her secretary. Establishing an initial rapport is important: you may have to enlist the secretary's aid.

First, give your name and ask for the person you want. 'This is Alex Smith. Can you put me through to Mr/Ms Ace?' This may gain you immediate access.

Often your target will be in a meeting, on the other line, out of town, etc and you will be asked to leave a message. Be prepared for that question. You might try:

- 'No thank you, it's a personal matter – I will try again later.'
- 'It's about a letter that I sent on the 23rd. Do you know if it was received?'
- 'Jill Jones, a mutual friend, suggested that I call.'

Persistence will be necessary. If your target always seems to be busy try asking when would be a good time to call. Frequently, a good time to phone busy executives is half an hour before or half an hour after the normal working day.

If you encounter a very protective secretary try to get her support by explaining your reason for calling and sell yourself. A PA or secretary who is protective probably knows a lot about the company. If you convince him/her, your chances of assistance are good.

Be prepared for the odd time when your target picks up the phone himself. Do not delay – go straight into your rehearsed speech.

You are going to get a large number of rejections. If you are referred to the personnel department try to salvage some advantage. Ask for the name of the person you should contact. You will then legitimately be able to claim, when you speak, 'Mr Ace told me to phone you concerning . . .'

Preparing for the Interview

The date and time have been set. You have achieved an important phase of your job search campaign; you have an interview.

Perhaps, unknown to you, your training has already prepared you for this next stage. Earlier I described the first interview as 'the initial skirmish'. This meeting calls for the same preparation:

- In-depth research/intelligence.
- Reconnaissance.
- Preparation of a plan.
- Rehearsals.

Research/Intelligence

Your target is in sight. You must now carry out in-depth research on the company to try to discover its real structure, its corporate identity, what it does and where it is going.

Research must be carried out to identify where you might fit into the organization and where your expertise could be used to help them. Is it an established position, a newly created position, or could you create a position for yourself?

Much of the information you had probably gathered through your previous research. You now want to enter it

AN INTELLIGENCE SUMMARY

Company A T Aloss, 23 Corporation Drive, New Town

Background A T Aloss designs and manufactures mechanical and electrical switches and components. These switches are incorporated into a great variety of high and low tech equipment.

Clients
1. Over 8000 companies in the UK use switches designed by the company.
2. Over 16,000 companies world-wide.
3. Aloss lies No 3 in the UK for manufacture of switches behind Acme Industries and Photon plc but is the leader in the development of electrical power breakers to the military and nuclear industry.

Mod	ChemNuc	Shell Oil	Ford UK	Air India
Fiat	Umlat GmbH	Offshore Oil	British Telecom	
SkySat	Bundesbahn	Brit Oil	The Natural Gas Co	
Brit Aerospace	Hanson plc	The Royal Bank of Scotland		

Profile A T Aloss 3rd largest manufacturer
Privately held
Increased sales last year 15%
Average annual growth 6%
1500 employees
Locations: Headquarters: Newtown
Factory: Glasgow
Offices: Reading (Berks)
La Vallange (Paris)
Unna (Dortmund)
Alicante
Opening new factory 92/93 Malta
Opening new office 93 Singapore

History: Company founded in 1954 by Alfred and Thomas Aloss in a rented warehouse near Pangbourne, Berks. Thomas died in 1978. Alfred Chairman of the Board (68), handed over as MD to son Alan (46) in 1989. Alan Aloss held Short Service Commission RE (70–74).

Notes Product depends upon rigorous inspection programme.

Co intends to expand further in Europe and wants to enter Far East market.

Co intends to reorganize distribution methods.

Logistics Director recently promoted to Operations Director.

See attached articles:

Figure 10 *Example of an Intelligence Summary*

Preparing for and Conducting the Interview

into an intelligence review, an example of which is shown in Figure 10.

Return to the public library and turn up any recent articles about your target company, its rivals and its product. What you are trying to find out about are the company's problems, knowledge of which you can use to your advantage. Enter the information in your Intelligence Summary.

If you have a friendly stockbroker and the company is trading on the Stock Exchange ask for a Stock Exchange EXTEL card on the company. This is a current, concise, financial summary on the company, which gives potential investors a recommendation on investing in that stock.

Review your network list and try to find someone who can give you an insight into the company. A current or ex-employee is ideal and the resultant conversation is likely to be most illuminating.

Try to visualize what this prospective employer might be wanting and select the experience, strengths and skills that you possess which might be appropriate.

Reconnaissance

You cannot afford to be late, so carry out a reconnaissance. Telephone the company and ask for advice and directions to the meeting.

If you can conduct a dry run, so much the better. It will help to reduce anxiety on the actual day.

If the meeting is at a distant location and you are travelling by car ask for advice from one of the motoring associations so as to avoid traffic delays and congestion. If you are travelling by train leave plenty of time. Rather than walking, splash out on a taxi; the cost will more than outweigh your arriving puffed, dishevelled and possibly soaked.

The plan

Examine your Intelligence Summary and make a tentative plan as to how you will conduct your side of the interview:

- What achievements and strengths do you want to bring out during the interview?
- What questions do you want to ask?
- What paperwork do you want to take?
- What information do you want to find out?

The rehearsal
Rehearsals are vital when preparing to meet people during a job-search campaign. This is a one-off situation in which you have a single chance to put over your personality, your experience, your enthusiasm and your suitability. Nothing should be left to chance, everything should be prepared for, including dress, introductions, your self-promotion, answers to questions, your body language and how you will conduct your side of the interview.

All meetings and interviews can be divided into five parts:

- Pre-interview action.
- Introductions and preliminaries.
- The interview.
- Closing the interview.
- Post-interview action.

The mechanics of dealing with each will be covered in subsequent paragraphs.

Telephone to confirm your attendance. Company executives are busy people and they will understand should you have to rearrange a meeting. If you do not know who will be conducting the interview, ask and get the name and position in the company of the interviewer.

Read and commit to memory the salient points of your Intelligence Summary.

Use an 8" × 6" card and prepare an interview plan. On this card enter the name, address and telephone number of the company, the name of the interviewer and the appointment time. Also note down the questions that you want to ask.

At some time during the interview you are almost sure to be asked, 'Tell me about yourself.' Review your two-minute self-advert and prepare a specific edition for this interview. Again it should not last more than two minutes and should be tailored to your analysis of the company's needs. Now practise the answer out loud, preferably into a tape recorder, so that you can hear how you sound. Keep on practising until the answer comes fluently, interestingly and seemingly unrehearsed.

In your plan for the interview you included the skills that you wish to communicate. Select anecdotes which demonstrate how you successfully employed these skills. Massage these anecdotes so that they are pithy, relevant and direct. Then rehearse them so that they appear to emerge naturally. You should be able to weave the story into the conversation somewhere in the interview. Everyone likes to hear a good story and the substance of a story will be remembered far longer than a list of your talents.

Think of and write down every question that might be asked during the interview. A few questions specific to the military are listed below. There is, however, an interesting book by Martin John Yate entitled *Great Answers to Tough Interview Questions* which covers this subject in depth (see Further Reading, page 118).

Prepare answers to all the questions you have posed and rehearse the answers using the tape recorder, for example.

Q. *'What are your weaknesses?*
This is a question designed to see how you respond under pressure. No one wants to reveal something that they do not do well. So choose a weakness and turn it round to reveal a strength.

A. 'I used to find it difficult to delegate my responsibility because often I felt that I could do it better myself, but I realized that it was only by delegating that I could train and improve the efficiency of those for whom I was responsible.'

Q. *'What have you done to civilianize yourself?'*
A question which reveals the worry that a potential employer may have that someone with a military background cannot adjust to the corporate way of life. Reveal that you have taken this into account when you identified your transferable skills.

A. 'I have been very fortunate to have learned and experienced much during my military career. I have identified those skills and experiences such as . . . [insert your own] . . . which I believe can contribute to the success of the company. I have also carried out in-depth research into the problems of . . . [insert one of the problem areas associated with that industry/service]. . . . I believe that my training in . . . [insert skill] . . . will provide fresh insight and produce a solution. Don't you agree?'

Q. *'Why did you leave?'*
This is a genuine question. It is asked to try to assess the value that your previous employer placed on you. Whatever the reason behind leaving the Services, you want to be positive and convey that the decision to leave was a conscious decision made by you.

A. 'The social and economic changes that have occurred over the last couple of years have produced wonderful opportunities for progressive companies. Although I could have continued in the Services I decided that the time was right and that I have the skills to make a positive contribution to the right company.'

Q. *'Are you receiving a pension?'*
While this question might be interpreted as getting closer to making you an offer, it is an absolute no no. Your compensation level should never reflect what you are getting from another source, ie an assumption that you can be got more cheaply because your pension will

make up the difference. Your pension is part payment of what you have contributed over previous years. Your compensation is in anticipation of the increased profits that you are going to make. Answer this question politely but briefly.

A. 'Yes, I do receive a pension for my 16 years' service.' Or: 'No, I left before I became eligible.'

Dress and personal appearance

Many of you will have worn a uniform to conduct your daily business. You will find that the suits, dresses and shoes that you have in your wardrobe to relax in or to wear to a social gathering are unsuitable for daily work or for interviews. You should, therefore, take the cost of purchasing your new 'uniform' into account.

Much has been said in the past about 'power dressing' or dressing to impress. While the way you dress is a demonstration of your personality, the interview is not the time to exercise this individuality, unless you are seeking a position in an artistic environment. The guidelines are that you should be comfortable and that your interviewer should be comfortable with you.

You are presenting yourself; therefore, you want to make a good impression without eliciting any adverse comment.

Personal appearance

Your hair should be clean and neat. Avoid growing a moustache or beard at this time.

Personal cleanliness must, of course, be of the highest standard but avoid also overuse of your favourite perfume or after-shave.

Never smoke during an interview. Immediately before a meeting, avoid smoking, drinking alcohol or eating anything very pungent that might stain your clothes or lodge between your teeth.

The Job Assault Course

Clothes
Your clothes should fit in with the environment; for most occasions this will be conventional business attire.

For men this will be a dark suit, usually blue or grey, with a conventional shirt and tie. Research has shown that shirts should be blue or white and ties either plain or striped. I believe that this convention is outdated. As long as the shirt and tie are clean, not frayed, and conservative, and you feel that they go with the suit you are the best judge.

For women there is a greater latitude. Wear what you feel smart in but avoid anything that is too tight, too low or too short.

Footwear should always be clean, in good repair and conventional.

Jewellery
Keep personal jewellery to a minimum.

Preparing for and Conducting the Interview

CHAPTER 8
The Interview

There are so many different types of interview that a list would be too long and cumbersome. I have, therefore, placed interviews into four categories:

- *The Networking Interview.* Where you are seeking information – covered in Chapter 5.
- *The Target Interview.* An interview with a decision maker in a company which you believe might create a job for you.
- *The Informal Interview.* This might be a meeting with a decision maker in an informal/social setting and at that time you do not know that you are being interviewed. These interviews can be fraught with danger; just remember the saying, 'A policeman is never off duty', and apply the same maxim to yourself.
- *The Job Interview.* Where you are being interviewed for a specific opening. Such interviews can include *Screening Interviews* either face-to-face or over the telephone, *Hiring Interviews* where a shortlist of candidates is being examined, or a *Confirmatory Interview* at which your new boss has made his decision but wants the nod of approval from *his* boss.

As mentioned earlier, an interview can be broken down into five constituent parts:

- Pre-interview action.
- Introductions and preliminaries.

The Interview

- The interview.
- Closing the interview.
- Post-interview action.

The purpose of this section is to explain each stage, prepare you, the interviewee, for your part in the interview process and offer some suggestions which might give you an edge over other candidates.

Some suggestions will be stating the obvious, others will, it is hoped, be of assistance.

Pre-interview Action

This phase of the interview process is probably the one when the nervousness and anxiety of the interviewee will be at their height. Fear of the unknown is always the worst. The tips given below, together with your preparation, will relax you so that you can be at your most effective.

Arrive at the interview location a few minutes early. There may be security or reception arrangements which will take a few minutes or the actual interview may be located in an adjoining building. You do not want to start your interview with an apology for being late.

Visit the lavatory. This will give you a chance to compose yourself, check your appearance and make yourself comfortable. Wash your hands; you will probably be slightly nervous and your palms may be sweating. This will ensure that you will be able to give a firm, dry handshake. Take three or four deep breaths which will calm you, then go to the receptionist.

Announce who you are and who you are seeing, then get rid of any unwanted paraphernalia such as hat, coat and umbrella. If you can, get rid of your briefcase, unless you have material that you wish to show. Remembering to extract writing material and a pen and perhaps a copy of your CV.

If you are asked to wait, read the company newsletter; you will be able to learn more about the company.

Keep alert and examine what is going on around you. Much can be learned of the company ethos through watching people at work. Note how people dress, how the telephone is answered. Is the atmosphere casual or formal, calm or chaotic, busy or slack, professional or amateur? Remember that you are trying to secure a job with this organization, therefore you will have to fit into its corporate image.

If you are offered a drink (usually tea or coffee) always accept even if you do not want one. When one is nervous the first sign is a dryness of the mouth. Sipping a beverage will prevent you croaking your way through your sales pitch.

Introductions and Preliminaries

This phase is the preliminaries before getting down to the business. The social conventions of almost every country dictate that there should first be some social exchange. Such exchanges may be short, as is the convention in the USA, or long as is the convention in Arab countries. It is the time when both parties examine each other and gauge the chemistry that the meeting releases. This is your chance to create a favourable first impression.

When you are called forward to meet your interviewer remember that first impressions do count. The impression you wish to convey is of a professional, self-confident person who is at ease in every situation. Think of all the people who gave you that kind of first impression. Without exception the common denominators were that they stood straight, looked you in the eye, had a smile on their face and gave you a firm handshake together with a forceful greeting.

Do not sit down until you are invited. When you do sit down, neither lounge in the seat nor perch on the edge. Assume a relaxed position but with a straight back.

Contribute to any polite, social chit-chat. The purpose is to help both parties to relax.

When the interviewer turns the conversation to the subject of your meeting end the social chit-chat, smile and become the professional that you are.

Body language is the unconscious motions that the body makes which transmit your actual feelings and emotions. Many professional interviewers attend courses in this subject as an adjunct to their interviewing skills. Everyone notices it in others but few recognize it in themselves. Some common examples include:

Avoiding eye contact – demonstrates discomfort, fear, boredom or shiftiness.
Mumbling – conveys lack of confidence or insecurity.
Incessant rubbing of hands – apology or discomfort.
Shifting of legs – nerves.
Closing of the eyes – deep thought or contemplation.

Recognizing that the human body does transmit inner feelings and following the guide lines given below will help to prevent the wrong message being interpreted.

- Get yourself into a comfortable position in the chair.
- Do not become immobile; the body naturally likes to move. Don't shift about; instead, lean forward when you are talking and lean back when you are listening.
- Look at the person when he/she is talking or take notes and try to keep your body still. You can nod your head occasionally.
- Use your hands naturally for emphasis but never fold your arms, grip your knees or cover your mouth or face.

The Interview

This is the moment that you have waited and prepared for. The company needs someone like you; all you have to do is persuade the interviewer that you are that person.

Interviewing is a technique which can be mastered. Of course, practice makes perfect. What you are trying to do is use your research, your qualities and skills and apply them to the requirements of the company in such a way as to convince the interviewer that you merit further consideration.

The interviewer is trying to find out whether you would fit into the company, whether you are qualified for the job and what you would contribute to the profitability of the organization.

The first rule is to listen closely to what the interviewer is saying.

The second rule is to pause before you reply in order to collect your thoughts and compose your reply. With luck, you will recall or adapt one of the answers that you rehearsed.

Rule three is to answer the question precisely, concisely, unhurriedly and audibly. Do not ramble or wander off the subject.

Rule four is to ask questions that show your knowledge of the company, its problems and what you can contribute. Do not list the problems you have found. Rather, phrase them in such a way that the interviewer will tend to tell you more specifics. You will then have an opportunity to use one of your prepared anecdotes, for example:

> You have found out that the organization has recently bought out a number of smaller competitors. A reasonable deduction would be that there is a problem with instilling a corporate spirit.
>
> Do not say, 'My expertise in team building will solve your morale problem.'
>
> Instead try, 'How did Ace Industries disseminate its corporate philosophy to its new acquisitions? I suspect it was quite difficult.'
>
> When you have listened to the reply you can come up with an anecdote which highlights your leadership and team-building qualities.

The fifth rule is not to bring up the subject of your needs too early in the interview procedure.

The last rule is to be more of a listener and learner than a talker.

Closing the Interview

There comes a time in every interview when you should progress to your plan for closing the interview. The time to start will be either instinctive or as scheduled, as in a networking interview where you have asked for 30 minutes.

This is the second last chance that you have to impress your interviewer. Your closing argument should, therefore, be powerful.

In the preceding paragraphs I have tried to show that you should not be the follower in the interview but an equal partner in the process. Do not let the initiative slip now.

Do not wait until the interviewer says, 'Well, thank you, Mr Jones. We will let you know. Goodbye.' You want to end the interview. You should thank the interviewer, leave him/her convinced of the strength of your candidacy, your keenness for the job and know what the next step in the process is.

When you feel that both sides have found out what they want to know, end by saying something like:

For a Network Interview. 'Gerald, thank you for your time. I am most grateful for your suggestions. As for the contacts you have offered me, should I contact them first and can I use your name or will you drop them a note? Thanks again, I will let you know how my search progresses.'

For a Targeted Interview. 'Mr Jackson, thank you for sparing me your time. I enjoyed hearing how you intend to deal with X and it matches almost exactly with my experience and with the research that I have carried out. If I may, I will drop you a note laying out the steps that I believe will contribute to solving the situation and give you a call next week. Goodbye.'

For an Informal Interview. 'Thank you for the drink and for your insight into X. That is exactly the sort of challenge I am seeking. Let me put down some ideas that have occurred to me on paper. I would like to give you a call next week.'

For a Job Interview. 'Thank you, Mr/Ms Bossbody. Your description of the future development of Acme is very exciting. I can see how important this position will be and that experience and knowledge in [insert the skills that you have matched] will be vital. This is exactly the type of challenge that I have been seeking and one where I can make an immediate contribution. What is the next step?' . . . [answer] . . . 'Right. I shall call you in a couple of days. Thank you again. I really enjoyed our meeting. Goodbye.'

Post-interview Action

This stage in the interview sequence is as important as any of the others and must take place within 24 to 48 hours after the interview.

- Before you leave ask at the reception for the names of those you met (remember to check how to spell the names), their titles and the postal address.
- Send a thank you note which includes mention of any matter that you promised to action. The thank you letter for a job interview is your last chance to affect the interviewer. Include enthusiasm for the position and how you are qualified for the post. See also under the heading 'Thank You Letters' in Chapter 6 (page 70).
- Debrief yourself on how you did during the interview. It is important to identify parts that you thought went well, those that went less well and any that were disastrous. This debriefing will help to pin-point areas that you will

POST-INTERVIEW DEBRIEF

Pre-Interview
Arrived on time Yes/No
Initial impression of workplace:
Initial impression of interviewer:
How did prelims go? Why?
Were you reasonably relaxed? Yes/No Why?

Interview
Did you handle the questions? Yes/No Why?
Did any questions faze you? Yes/No Why?
Did you put over your skills? Yes/No Why?
Do you know all about the position? Yes/No Why?
Did the interview stay on track? Yes/No Why?
Did you achieve your aim? Yes/No Why?

Body language OK?
   Smile:
   Hand-shake:
   Relaxed:
   Posture:
   Fidgeting:
   Arms natural:
   Eye contact:

Aural technique OK?
   Listened to question:
   Interrupted:
   Forget question:
   Lost track:
   Eye contact:

Verbal technique OK?
   Volume.
   Varied pitch:
   Speed:
   Thought before you spoke:
   Emphasized your points:
   Matched the interviewer:
   Used trite or hackneyed phrases:
   Umm'd and err'd:
   Monotonous:

Interview technique OK?
   Got the name right:
   Used the prepared anecdotes:
   Introduced your skills:
   Matched skills to needs:
   Let knowledge of organization show:
   Kept to time frame:

Closing the Interview
Did you retain the initiative? Yes/No Why?
Did you put over your enthusiasm? Yes/No Why?
Do you know what happens next? Yes/No Why?

Figure 11 *An Example of Post-interview Debrief*

have to include in future rehearsals. A guide is laid out in Figure 11.
- Update all the information you gathered about the company and its needs and about the job and its requirements. Enter this information in your Intelligence Summary to prepare for your next interview.

If the interview was an absolute shambles, do not despair. The experience will significantly improve your future performance.

If the job does not sound like what you want, or the company does not appear to be one that you would like to work for, do not rule it out immediately. If you were offered the job perhaps you could alter some of the less attractive aspects during negotiations. You are also receiving good interview practice. You are learning a tremendous amount about a competitor should you try to land another job in the same industry. Continue to interview until you are struck off or are offered the job.

If the interview went well, start your preparation but do not slow down your overall campaign.

Interview Techniques

Interviewing is an art form; in some ways it resembles a play with a definite purpose but a loose plot. To take this analogy further, both you and the interviewer are actors working from a free-flowing script. Actors learn techniques to enhance their natural abilities. Similar techniques can be used to improve interviewing style.

Aural techniques
Listening is an important part of an interview. Remember that you need information if you are going to be able to convince the hirer that you are the right person for the task.

Being a good listener sends important signals to the interviewer. It conveys seriousness, intelligence, maturity and knowledge.

Eye contact. When being interviewed, maintain frequent eye contact with the interviewer when he/she is speaking. Eye contact reinforces that you are listening to what is being said. It also encourages the speaker to continue.

Mannerisms. Humans use mannerisms to emphasize that they are paying attention. Their use encourages the speaker and creates a bond and a lasting impression. The mannerisms include smiling, nodding the head, cocking the head to one side, frowning as if in concentration, raising the eyebrows, sitting back and the taking of notes. If you carried out each of the litany of mannerisms given above, throughout the interview, you might be taken for an escapee from an institution. However, judicious use of these common mannerisms will enhance your interview technique.

Paying close attention. Only by paying attention to what is being said will you be able to pick up the nuances to help you phrase the right answers in response to questions. Key statements will emerge during a conversation which reveal what the speaker believes to be important. You should try to re-use these statements in your response. Note important facts and statements down as they occur. If the interviewer is interrupted in mid-flow, for example, by a telephone call, note where the conversation had reached so that you can quickly resume the dialogue. Your attention will be appreciated.

The use of silence. Silence is an important weapon. When used with the appropriate body language it can signify disagreement, dissent, deep thought or encouragement. Accompanied by a smile, use silence to encourage the interviewer to further explain an important aspect of policy.

Verbal techniques
Speech not only conveys information, it also transmits impressions. I believe that a good speaker can put over a

boring subject but a boring speaker can seldom maintain an audience's attention, whatever the subject.

Good speakers use verbal techniques to help them hold the attention of their audience.

Volume and pitch. You must be able to be heard to be understood. However, speaking too loudly is wearing on the listener. Raising and lowering your voice and modulating the intonation and pitch will significantly enhance your delivery. If all this sounds too much, record your voice. If you sound boring, rehearse.

Enunciating. Speak slowly and clearly and try to match the way your interviewer speaks. Do not use long words, trite or hackneyed phrases and avoid umm's and err's.

General techniques

Ensure that you get names and titles right. If you are attending an interview with more than one interviewer, take the time to write down the names. Check the spelling with the receptionist before you leave.

Avoid posing questions where the answer can only be yes or no.

Find out the job requirements as early in the interview as you can. This will enable you to relate your strengths to the company needs from the beginning.

Keep an eye on the time. You must have time to put over your strengths and your personality before you enter the wind-up phase.

Try to get a follow-up interview before you leave. At least learn what the next step in the process is.

The Interview

CHAPTER 9
Dealing with Depression and Kick Starting a Stalled Search

Dealing with Depression

When a job search takes more than a few months there will be ups and downs and periods of depression.

Many of you will never have been out of work before. However many times one has been on one's own and had to exercise personal responsibility, been given tasks with insufficient support or had to motivate oneself to complete a thankless and seemingly endless task, been frightened and unsure, nothing has prepared the first-time jobless for the rigours of conducting a job-search campaign.

There is no one to support you, save your immediate family. Advice, however well meaning, is often conflicting. There is nothing to measure your success against. Thus, when faced with rejection or a search that seems to lead nowhere, there is a danger that you will take this setback personally and allow depression to set in.

Depression can manifest itself in many ways: a shortness of temper with your family; the loss of self-respect leading to an erosion of self-confidence; a change in your sleeping habits leading to nights of restless worry; a slipping of your personal standards such as not getting dressed in the morning; a general lethargy allowing you to put off what you know you should do today until later in the week. Whatever the manifestation of depression, it must be banished quickly to allow you to get back on track.

Questions from friends

Initially your friends will ask you, 'How is the search going?' After a remarkably short time this can turn into 'What, still out of work!' This is usually not malicious but a reflection of the memories of the boom years and a lack of understanding of the current situation. For the first time a huge number of senior and middle managers and white-collar workers are out of work. Not all the problems can be laid at the door of the recession. Modern management techniques aided by computerization have necessitated a shift in management style to reflect the need to remain competitive.

The effect of the 1990/92 recession is that there has been a slow-down in the capital available to companies to expand or start up new ventures. The signs are that this is changing. There are plenty of jobs being created each day and the modern manager can no longer be insular with limited horizons. Instead he/she must have a breadth of talents including being able to assume responsibility, motivate, show leadership and take a global perspective. These skills are developed in the military environment possibly better than in any other.

There is no stigma attached to looking for a job – only in not looking. Answer your friends positively, not defensively. No, you have taken any old job – you are looking for the right job!

If friends stop being 'friends'

You may notice a change in attitude among some whom you thought were friends. The telephone stops ringing, the invitations stop coming in and, worst of all, friends cross the street to avoid you. The actions of those few can be very hurtful. They possibly do not mean it and it stems from their own fears for their job security.

Provided that you are focused on what you want and do not wear out your friendship with undirected requests for networking help, your true friends will remain a constant source of inspiration and help.

Beware of the no nos
Depression is a result of succumbing to what I have called the no nos.

Not following your plan
The early part of this book was devoted to analysing your requirements, identifying your skills and preparing a plan of campaign. When you lose this focus you lose direction. When you lose direction you become aimless. When you become aimless you become depressed.

Letting your standards slip
You have developed personal standards over the years which have made you what you are. If you allow those standards to slip you lose part of yourself. Your inner self will know this and your moral fibre will be undermined.

Get up at the time you always rose. Dress smartly for the tasks that you have set yourself that day.

Do not allow yourself that other drink. Who knows when the telephone may ring. You certainly cannot afford to sound smashed.

Exercise regularly. You will probably put on a little weight if you have exchanged a highly active lifestyle for a more sedentary one, but let it only be a little weight for you need to be fit and alert for the job search.

Never become a couch potato in front of the afternoon TV.

Do not give up your hobbies. They not only help you to relax and refresh your spirits but they are where you will meet people.

Do not forget your family; plan an outing, take a break together. Go out to the cinema, a restaurant or a football match. Remember that your campaign is a team effort and you all deserve a reward for your hard work.

Avoiding the 'dear trap'
Your presence at home during the day is a novelty. You may have only recently moved to a new house or reoccupied

yours after it has been rented out for years. Establish that you are in your office, not at your home; they are only the same place during the period of your search. So avoid the dear trap:

'Dear, could you help with the shopping?'
'Dear, could you paint the dining room?'
'Dear, could you look after the baby/dog/workmen?'

Kick Starting a Stalled Search

You have run out of ideas, your leads have dried up and your campaign has stalled. You feel the onset of depression. It is time to kick start your search.

Redefine your goals
Examine your self-analysis exercise and confirm that the goals you seek are realistic. It is to be hoped that they remain true. If not, redefine them. You will probably find that you have missed some aspect that your new-found experience will tell you is important.

Rejig your CV
Examine your CV with a critical eye. Does it promote you? Does it answer a company's needs? Have you left out a skill which is in demand? Is it eye-catching or boring? Sit down and reshape it in the light of experience.

Find new resources
Search your network list. Did you follow up on all the leads or did you give up on some? Is it worth returning to an early contact because you are now more focused? Who else do you know who might be willing to help? What about that former Squadron Commander of yours who left five years ago? It is impossible to exhaust all your contacts if you have been carrying out a well-planned campaign. You only have to think hard.

The Job Assault Course

Refining the plan

Review your campaign plan. Where did it get stalled and why? Return to the library and research new companies.

Go to the local Chamber of Commerce and find out the names of companies who import or export or are foreign owned. Find out the names of companies who have been granted building permission or who have bought up other companies – they are expanding. Find out the names of troubled companies – they might need your managerial experience. Make a note of companies who have grown from small to medium and might have outgrown the experience of their founders.

Whatever you do, get out, find new leads and refine your plan.

"Options For Change" - The Next Move?
We can help you find a new job

Directors / Senior Managers

- Specialists in "Options for Change" redundancy placements
- Professional outplacement and career consultants to maximise your potential
- Get the right job through access to the unadvertised job market
- Quality services, without frills, include one-to-one counselling
- Programmes approved for interest free Government loan scheme

For free initial consultation call
LONDON 071 379 3133.   DORKING 0306 888522

HEADWAY
Old King's Head Court, High Street, Dorking, Surrey RH4 1AR

Headway adheres to the IPM Code of Conduct for Career and Outplacement Consultants.

'So you have decided to leave and do some real work.'

CHAPTER 10
The Negotiations, the Offer and the Signing

In Chapter 5 I described Phase 5 of your job-search campaign as 'the offer and the terms of the treaty'. During the interview process there will come a time when you sense that you are being thought of as a serious candidate. You are close to reaching your goal and being offered a position within the company/organization.

You have succeeded in selling yourself to the hiring manager. He/she thinks that you are a desirable commodity who will increase profits which will probably far outweigh the compensation that you will receive. You are no longer chasing the job; the job is chasing you.

You are now entering the difficult area of negotiation, a window of opportunity where you can explore, haggle and try to get what you want. This opportunity does not last long and you must be prepared to seize it when it appears. The purpose of this chapter is to help you to not sell yourself short and to negotiate and close a satisfactory compensation package.

Negotiations

The reason for negotiation
Compensation negotiations pave the way to a contract of employment. Rather like a treaty or pact in international diplomacy they hammer out an agreement equable to both sides. There is a fine balance:

The Negotiations, the Offer and the Signing

- You do not want to feel that you have been bought too cheaply as this will be a source of resentment.
- The company does not want you to feel dissatisfied as they know that you will jump ship the moment a better offer comes along.
- The company does not want to feel that they must pay too high a price or this will sour relations and make the runner-up start to look more attractive.
- You do not want to have negotiated too high a compensation package because the company might not close the deal, your co-workers might resent you and too much pressure may be placed upon you to justify your high compensation.

Thus the purpose of the negotiations is to arrive at a mutually satisfactory package. Of course, your bargaining power is dependent upon a number of things:

- How valuable your skills are to the company.
- How many other candidates there are.
- How you feel about negotiating.
- How desperate you are.

Whatever your personal circumstances, remember that you are a commodity which is in demand and that whatever the company's stated policy on pay may be, there is always room for negotiation.

What is open for negotiation

You may notice that I have used the words *compensation* and *package* rather than pay or salary. Your base salary is only one factor in your overall compensation package.

Listed in Figure 12 are some components of an overall package which may be up for negotiation. In many cases they add up to over 40 per cent on top of the base salary.

What you want to end up with is a package which suits your personal circumstances.

The Job Assault Course

THE COMPENSATION PACKAGE

Basic salary	Expense account
Bonus	Reimbursement of:
Profit sharing	moving expenses
	mortgage penalty
Company car and petrol	legal expenses
Paid holidays	bridging loan interest
	house-hunting expenses
Share options/assisted share purchase	Overseas travel/spouse travel
Company pension scheme	Children's education costs
Additional voluntary contributions	Executive dining-room
	Club membership
Private health plan	Low interest loan
Life assurance	Access to tax accountant
Spouse life assurance	Post-termination insurance benefits
Sickness and disability pay	
Termination notice and pay	Legal assistance

Figure 12 *Negotiations: The Compensation Package*

Preparing for the negotiations

Sit down with your campaign team and list what you know about the pay structure of the company. If you know nothing seek advice.

- Certain jobs have pay bands listed in their industry journals.
- Ask your network what others in comparable positions are paid.
- You will be paid less than your boss but more than a subordinate.

The Negotiations, the Offer and the Signing

- Ask during one of your interviews – preferably not the screening interview.

This research will reveal a rough negotiating range. Decide on two check-points: the position below which you will not negotiate and another, higher up the scale, where the lack of base salary can be made up with perks and bonuses.

If the job is an established position you will know that there is a pay band within which there can be negotiation. If it is a new or specially created post serious compensation negotiations will have to take place.

During the early stages of your search you will have decided on the lowest offer that you will accept. In theory, therefore, anything over this threshold is gravy. Examine the list in Figure 12 and decide what must be included for your satisfaction. Prepare a list of what you would like to have included in your package, for example:

Must include: Bonus, medical insurance, moving expenses, pension.
Like to have: Company car, severance pay, life insurance, profit sharing.

Keep this wish list with you when you go to the interview.

Recognizing the moment to open negotiations
There are signs which indicate that you have successfully sold yourself and that you will soon have a chance to ask for what you want:

- You are called back for subsequent interviews.
- The interview runs over its allotted time.
- The interviewer starts a heavy sell of the company attributes.
- The interviewer raises the subject of specific salary and benefits.
- The conversation turns to your references or a medical examination.

These indicate that an offer is about to be made. The best time to open negotiations is following an offer and before acceptance.

It is possible to open discussion on compensation too early, ie before you have successfully sold yourself. Similarly, it is also possible to sour the deal by waiting too long, ie reopening negotiations after the deal has been sealed.

It is too late to renegotiate after you have started work. You must also cease negotiations when you perceive that you have got all that the company is willing to offer.

The Offer

When a job offer is made
Having been offered the position the first response might be:

> 'Mr/Ms Boss, I appreciate the confidence that you have shown in me by offering me this position. I believe that I have a firm grasp of what Acme Industries wants from me and I am excited at the prospect. Is this an appropriate time for discussion about the compensation package?'

At this time you should produce your wish list and start bringing up anything that you need most and explain why.

The secret to successful negotiating lies in using those skills employed by a diplomat:

> Tact, patience, determination and powerful persuasion. A willingness to concede points that are not fundamental. Thorough research and knowing what you want and how far to push. The ability to balance the needs of the company and yourself.

Negotiating salary and bonus
Negotiating the base salary is probably the most important

factor for both sides. Sometimes the subject of salary is raised at the first meeting to ensure that you are within the company's budget. One way of assessing your worth, perhaps unfairly, is by asking what you were earning previously.

You can hardly not reveal what you earned previously, but if you were on a fixed pay band, such as exists in the military, you should think about enhancing the base pay by including those intangibles which make up the complete package, namely: pay; skills pay; allowances – include school allowance if applicable; free clothing – you will now have to buy your work clothes; travel allowance, etc.

If the subject of salary is raised too early, and you are trying for a substantial increase over your last pay cheque, sow the seed but try not to get locked into a pay scale too early. Say something along the lines of:

> 'The pay scale laid down for someone of my rank is around .... I am hoping that my move to Acme Industries will be a progressive step. I also feel that, provided we are thinking along similar lines about the outline pay for this job, perhaps we should postpone discussion on the compensation package until we have discussed some of the other factors such as the responsibilities of this position and the future intentions of the company.'

If a bonus is an important part of the overall package, you must determine how it is assessed and what size it has been over the last few years. If it is linked to your performance, you will need to determine what resources you will be given and what limitations are placed on it.

If pay is a sticking point try to negotiate other ways to increase your salary.

- If the company say that your starting salary will be subject to an annual review, try to get agreement that your first review will take place after six months in the job.

- Try to enlarge the responsibilities of the job, which will justify an increased salary.

Benefits and perquisites
Benefits can contribute significantly to the total worth of your compensation package. Some perks may have little intrinsic value, but may impart prestige, such as a named parking space. Other non-financial perks, such as a car, may have significant cash or tax benefits but note that there are now fewer perks with tax benefits than there were before.

Relocation costs are significant and many expenses are negotiable. The out-of-pocket expenses incurred in moving, such as packing and removal, hotel costs and changing the children's school, can cost many hundreds of pounds. The biggest expense can be selling and buying a home. Before becoming locked into accepting a new job, assess the cost and include a study of house prices.

Financial assistance for relocation will depend on the company's policy, any precedent and how much the company wants you. You should raise the subject during negotiations. If the sticking point is precedent consider asking for a lump sum, the so-called hiring bonus.

The Signing

Closing the deal
When you have concluded negotiations, again express your thanks for the offer and your eagerness for the challenge. Unless you are absolutely sure about all aspects, sign nothing at this stage.

If the negotiations have not been satisfactory, do not close the door on the deal by saying 'Thanks but no thanks'. Instead keep the negotiations open by saying something like:

> 'Ms Boss, thank you again for the job offer. It is a job that I know I could do well and I would very much like working for this company. Unfortunately, ... seems to

The Negotiations, the Offer and the Signing

be a sticking point which I will have to think about seriously. I would like us to keep in touch.'

This will allow you both time to consider and possibly open further negotiations.

If the negotiations have been satisfactory, verbally accept the position and ask for the offer to be made in writing. If this is not normal company practice, say that you would like time to think about the offer/talk it over with your partner. The period should not exceed 48 hours.

Although you have exchanged a verbal contract in a strictly legal sense, your contract is only enforceable when you exchange written agreements. Horror stories abound where an offer has been accepted only for the company to renege before the deal has been signed.

The final analysis

This thinking period could be important to you. You are freed of the euphoria of landing the job and you can examine the job offer in detail. Sit down and think about all the aspects of the job, the things you like and the things you do not, including:

The job itself –	Your responsibilities, ie your mission.
	Who you report to.
	Who reports to you.
	The level of authority you have.
The company –	Its stability – you do not want to enlist in a sinking ship.
	Its current and future plans.
	Its competitors.
Work environment –	The type of boss you have.
	The management style.
	The cultural style.
	The future for you.

The compensation

What the job means to your family.

When you have analysed all the factors you can decide whether to accept the offer.

If you have been sent the offer in writing or a work contract, sign it and return it with a covering letter. If the offer is still only verbal, write a letter accepting the offer and include all the details that you negotiated in your compensation package. When you start work it will be too late to find out that the person you negotiated with did not have the authority to agree to some of your requirements.

Once you have exchanged written offers you have in effect a contract. If for some reason the job offer has to be withdrawn you can argue for compensation.

The final touch

Following your celebration of the successful conclusion of your job-search campaign, help your new employer with any PR that he/she may wish to release. Then start informing people of your new circumstances. Write a polite letter to any companies where you had interviews. Write or telephone everyone in your network who has helped you and the search firms where you were listed.

Maintain close contacts with your network. It will still be the source of new ideas, trends in industry and, in a couple of years, lead to new opportunities in your next campaign.

The Negotiations, the Offer and the Signing

PUB MANAGEMENT
Here's another interesting way to be loyal to the Crown and the Prince of Wales.

Loyalty and commitment are just two of the qualities necessary for running a successful Chef and Brewer pub or pub restaurant. We are looking for management couples who can also think on their feet, get on well with all kinds of people, and work hard.

It may not suit everyone, but if you think you can balance developing and running a busy retail outlet with providing the best possible standards of service to our customers, you could manage one of our 1400 houses around the UK.

Our comprehensive 10 week training course will equip you with many of the skills you'll need to manage an outlet of your own, provided you have a friendly, outgoing personality, drive, determination, and plenty of initiative.

An attractive salary and benefits package includes accommodation once you've been appointed to a pub. But perhaps the greatest reward is the satisfaction of a demanding job well done.

To find out more please write to: The Personnel Department, The Chef & Brewer Group Ltd., 106 Oxford Road, Uxbridge, Middlesex UB8 1NA. Tel. 0895 258233.

THE CHEF & BREWER GROUP
— LIMITED —
THE UK'S LEADING PUB & PUB RESTAURANT COMPANY

CHAPTER 11
The First Few Months in the Job

Although during your career you have moved jobs frequently, they have been with the same 'firm' where the same ground rules apply. The first few weeks of your new job require careful planning. At a time when you are anxious to surge ahead and get on with the job, you are under close scrutiny. Your boss is sizing you up to see whether you will measure up to his/her expectations. Your peers and subordinates are getting the feel of what it is going to be like working with you. First impressions do count; an initial unsympathetic reaction can take a long time to dispel.

This chapter may help you to become assimilated quickly within your new work environment.

Getting It Right

Research the goals
Soon after you start work seek an appointment with your boss. At this meeting review the tasks and goals that you are to deal with and find out the boss's priorities.

Carry out a diary check and enter any briefings, tours, presentations or semi-social gatherings that are planned. If there are none planned seek advice about who or what you should see to give you the best introduction to the company.

Book a time about two weeks ahead when you can outline your plan to the boss.

New broom syndrome

Avoid the temptation to change too much too fast. Allow for a period where you can examine how things have been done and ask people to explain why they are done that way. This will focus your attention on what needs changing and what should be retained.

Gather your team about you and review the goals and tasks that you have discussed with the boss. Ask for suggestions and listen to input from your team. This will achieve three things. It will focus the team on your priorities; it will establish that you believe in teamwork; and it will give you an insight into how competent, cooperative and creative your team is.

Plan and develop a strategy

Make a plan of how you are going to achieve your target. Present this plan to your boss and emphasize any changes that you may envisage, especially if they involve shifting personnel.

Clear all details of your plan with the boss. Until you have established your relationship with him/her you do not want to have any misunderstandings.

Clarify the method which you should use to make progress reports. Does the boss like written reports, formal presentations, weekly meetings or an informal chat? Whatever the preferred method it should be followed with a written record of decisions.

The old bore

Never criticize how things were conducted or handled by the previous administration. You do not know the problems that were faced, the people who were involved or what loyalties you are challenging.

Avoid observing how much better a problem was tackled in the Services. It is irrelevant, irritating and boring.

Office politics

Every organization has its internal politics – who is 'in', who is 'out', who is a 'doer', etc. It will take some time for you to identify the rising star in the internal politics of the company. Avoid becoming aligned with any faction until you are in a position to judge who is influential.

Working together in the Services and working together in the civilian world are different. There is less camaraderie and less tolerance outside the Service. Nowadays people are very aware of social issues. Avoid making any references, especially in jest, to sex, race or religion – which are obvious – but also smokers'/non-smokers' rights, the fur trade, animal rights, shooting, hunting and any other contentious issue.

This does not mean that you cannot hold a personal opinion, only that in the early stages, until you understand the corporate atmosphere, you should avoid accidental alienation.

Professional education

Consider joining local professional organizations, both informal and formal groups. The formal groups will have considerable support facilities on all aspects of your new career. The informal organizations will enable you to meet other professionals and enlarge your network.

Maintain the network that you so diligently built up during your job-search campaign. The members will prove a long-lasting source of help, inspiration, information and leads. Remember the old axiom, 'It's not *what* you know but *who* you know that counts'.

Conclusion

There is nothing that cannot be achieved provided there is a will to succeed and you are given the right tools for the job.

Servicemen and women are a product of perhaps the finest selection and teaching organization in the country. They have been taught to obey but not blindly; to accept responsibility and be accountable to others; to solve problems through analysis and logic; to lead by example and

The Job Assault Course

succeed by motivating others. Such skills and training are sorely needed in the corporate world.

What has not been taught is how to job hunt and how to translate the experience and skills learned. By finishing this book you have given yourself the right tools for the job. By using these tools and allying them to your own energy and determination you will soon complete the job assault course and find the prize that you seek and successfully make the transition from uniform to suit.

Bibliography

Ask your librarian for the most recent editions of the following titles, which would be expensive to buy:

Business Directories and Company Information

Britain's Top 2000 Private Companies, Jordan & Sons Ltd, 21 St Thomas Street, Bristol BS1 6JS.
Extel Statistical Services, Extel, 37–45 Paul Street, London EC2A 4PB.
Jordan's Business Reports, Jordan's Business Information Service; address above.
Kelly's Business Directory, annual, Windsor Court, East Grinstead House, East Grinstead, West Sussex RH19 1XB.
Key British Enterprises, annual, Dun & Bradstreet Ltd, Holmers Farm Way, High Wycombe, Bucks HP12 4UL.
Kompass Register, Kompass Publishers Ltd, Windsor Court, East Grinstead House, East Grinstead, West Sussex RH19 1XD.
Principal International Businesses, annual, Dun & Bradstreet; address above.
Sell's Directory of Products and Services, annual, Sell's Publications Ltd, 55 High Street, Epsom, Surrey KT19 8DW.
The Stock Exchange Official Year Book, annual, Macmillan Publishers Ltd, Houndmills, Basingstoke, Hampshire RG21 2XS.
The Times 1000, Times Books Ltd, 77–85 Fulham Palace Road, London W6 8JB.
Who Owns Whom, annual, Dun & Bradstreet; address above.

Books on Employment

Employment Gazette, Department of Employment; on subscription, monthly, HMSO.
Executive Post, Dudley House, Upper Albion Street, Leeds LS2 8PN.
Getting There: Jobhunting for Women, 2nd edn, 1990, Margaret Wallis, Kogan Page.
Going Freelance, 3rd edition, 1991, Godfrey Golzen, Kogan Page.
Great Answers to Tough Interview Questions, 3rd edition, 1992, Martin John Yate, Kogan Page.
The Mid-Career Action Guide, 2nd edition, 1992, Derek Kemp and Fred Kemp, Kogan Page.
Moving Up: A Practical Guide to Career Advancement, 1991, Stan Crabtree, Kogan Page.
Returning to Work: A Practical Guide for Women, 1989, Alec Reed, Kogan Page.
Working Abroad: The Daily Telegraph Guide, 15th edn, 1992, Godfrey Golzen, Kogan Page.
Start and Run a Profitable Consulting Business, Douglas A Gray, 1989, Kogan Page.

Books Published in the United States of America

Business information
Billion Dollar Directory: America's Corporate Families, Dun & Bradstreet, New York.
The National Job Bank, Bob Adams Inc, Boston, MA.
Standard & Poor's Register of Corporations, Director and Executives, Standard & Poor/McGraw-Hill, New York.
Thomas Register of American Manufacturers, Thomas Publishing, New York.

Employment
Access, National Association of Personnel Consultants, Washington, DC.

Bibliography

Career Employment Opportunities Directory, Ready Reference Press, Santa Monica, CA.

Career Guide to Professional Associations: A Directory of Organizations by Occupational Field, Carroll Press, Cranston, RI.

Executive Employment Guide, Management Information Service, New York.

Federal Career Opportunities, Federal Research Service Inc, Vienna, VA.

Federal Job Information Centers Directory, Office of Personnel Management, Washington, DC.

Federal Jobs, US Government Printing Office, Leesburg, VA.

Knock 'em Dead With Great Answers to Tough Interview Questions, Martin John Yate, Bob Adams Inc, Boston, MA.

Resumes that Knock 'em Dead, Martin John Yate, Bob Adams Inc, Boston, MA.

What Color is Your Parachute?, Richard Nelson Bolles.